— Definition of a Health Nut

A Health Nut is a person who is so wrapped up in healthful living that no matter what the subject of your conversation is, he will insert something into it that will bring it back to the topic of health.

Benny

Good health

Tony Cruciei

Published by:

Far North Publishing
1317 W. Northern Lights Blvd.
Box 624
Anchorage, AK 99503

Printed in the U.S.A.

Library of Congress Catalog Card Number
98-92707

ISBN: 0-9663383-0-8

Notice

The author is not a medical doctor. Be sure to consult with your physician prior to commencing any treatment.

The things the author mentions in this book are not substitutes for any treatment your doctor has prescribed. All health matter should have medical supervision.

Whenever there is anything wrong with me I immediately go to a doctor and incorporate his suggestions with what I have learned from my reading of health books.

Acknowledgement

I wish to thank all the writers of the many health books I have read and mentioned in this book that have made my life so much richer and enjoyable.

This book is dedicated to my sisters who I have missed so much these many years that we have been apart.

TABLE OF CONTENTS

TO BETTER ENJOY THIS BOOK
START READING ON PAGE 24
AND SAVE THIS CHAPTER ON
ROSE FOR LAST

1995
Rose

I would call my sister, Rose, on the telephone every once in a while to see how she was doing. With each call, she seemed to get more despondent. The doctors had diagnosed her as having Parkinsons, and her arthritis was getting progressively worse. I told her that I had learned a lot about healing and was going to come back to Pittsburgh to see if I could help to cure her arthritis. I figured that I would put Rose on a juice fast, using the grapefruit method, as described in the book, fresh vegetable and fruit juices. I thought that with the juice, vitamin supplements, and a complete change of diet, I would be able to help her. That was my plan as I boarded the plane for Pittsburgh.

As I sat, trying to doze off, and the plane got closer and closer to Pittsburgh, I realized that Rose wouldn't be able to go on a juice fast.

Rose was now seventy years old and, in the poor health that she was in, there was no way that she could stand such an ordeal. Plus, the way I had suffered on my first juice diet might kill her.

When I arrived in Pittsburgh I stayed at Martha's house to rest up, visit, and get over my jet lag. I then went to the most logical place there was, to find a naturopathic doctor to see if anything could be done for Rose. A wonderful girl at The East End Food Co-Op gave me the name and phone number of a Dr. G. I called Dr. G up and, after explaining the situation to her receptionist on the phone, made an appointment to go and talk to the doctor.

As I sat in the waiting room, I couldn't help looking at a woman also waiting. She was talking with her girlfriend. Her talk was normal, in fact the only thing different about her was that her hands trembled with the palsy, which is associated with Parkinsons.

When I met Dr. G, she turned out to be a real delight. She was friendly and cheerful and she assured me that she could do a lot for Rose. She told me she had worked with many arthritis and Parkinsons sufferers. She told me that on Saturday, which was four days from then, after her day's work at her office, she would drive the ten miles to McKeesport to see Rose.

When I arrived at Rose's, I was shocked at the change in her appearance in just the one year since my last visit. She was dressed in a bathrobe, her complexion was pasty white, and she shuffled along with aid of a walker.

After a hug and kiss, I sat on the sofa and she proceeded to tell me of her misery. She told of how the arthritis was crippling her. She said that when her daughters came to visit, all she could talk about was how much she was suffering. All of that kind of talk got them so depressed that they soon started keeping their visits to a minimum.

I told her that the next time they came to visit she should try to act more cheerful and they would come around more often. But I knew that if I was in her place I would act the same way. It's hard to act cheerful with all of that pain and misery.

I told her that the doctor was coming in four days and we wouldn't change any of her habits until she talked to the doctor. I also told her to keep the doctor's visit a secret from her daughters until we could show them some positive results.

Rose then told me about her eating habits. She said that, because of the pain, she gave up cooking. For a long time she lived on doughnuts, popcorn, and candy. She said that things were better now because she had signed up for Meals on Wheels. Meals on Wheels is where, for a minimal fee, they bring a prepared meal to your house every day. I think that most of it was paid for by the state from their earnings off of the state lottery.

During our wait for Saturday, the day of the doctor's arrival, I assisted Rose in every way I could. She took about nine drugs every day and I started getting them for her.

She would wear a diaper to bed at night, and before she went to bed she would ask me to bring her one of her sleeping pills. She had two different kinds. She had gotten one each from two different doctors, and each night she would tell me which one she wanted. Because of the combination of the sleeping pill, her weakened kidneys, and her general weakness, she had a hard time getting out of bed to go to the bathroom. I bought a little bell for her to ring when she wanted to go to the bathroom.

I slept in the bedroom next to hers, and whenever I heard the bell I would jump out of bed and hurry over to help her. This happened at least three times a night. When she was done in the bathroom, she would use her walker to shuffle herself back to her room. Once there, I would help her put a new diaper on and then help her to get positioned back in bed. Because of her sore back, she slept mostly on her side, and this was very uncomfortable for her. She would sit on the edge of the bed and I would swing her legs up and onto it. Then I would shift her body around until she was halfway comfortable. That was my nightly routine for the rest of my stay with Rose.

In the mornings, I would find Rose sitting in her reclining chair in the living room. When her sleeping pill had worn off, I guess she had enough energy to get out of bed, go to the kitchen and make coffee, then sit in her chair, waiting for me to get up.

I would make her breakfast of whatever she

requested and bring it to her, after which I would do the dishes. Then I would bring her the drugs that she was taking as she requested them all during the day.

At noon the Meals on Wheels would arrive and, when I looked at those meals, I sometimes almost gagged. The meat would usually be fatty ham smothered with thick gravy, or some chops, and then some greasy looking chicken legs. There was a lot of other things with the meals. This included potatoes prepared in several different ways with plenty of butter or margarine to put on them. There was usually some wilted looking vegetable or salad to go with it. Also, there was some cereal and a carton of milk for the next day's breakfast. For desert there was jello, cookies, or a piece of cake. There were also two pieces of white bread.

Once a week a woman paid for by the state would come in and clean the house for Rose. She would also help Rose take a shower. Since the woman only came in once a week, and Rose needed a bath more often than that, she soon lost her inhibitions and asked me to help her take a bath. I would help her get into the tub, which had a chair she sat in, while she took a shower. I helped wash her back and hair, then I helped her out of the shower.

Finally, Saturday came. Just before the doctor was scheduled to arrive, two of Rose's daughters entered the door accompanied each with one of their children. I had forgotten that Rose was the one sister in the family that couldn't keep a secret. When they called to see how she was doing, she just had to tell them about the doctor's visit to the house. Of course, they insisted on being there when the doctor arrived.

Dr. G was very nice to the girls and she greeted Rose very warmly. She told Rose that she had worked with many people with Parkinsons and that, if she took the supplements and the other things that she had brought with her, I would see a big improvement in her condition before I went back to Alaska. Dr. G told Rose that she would eventually be able to drive a car again.

From my previous talk with her, Dr. G realized that I knew what foods to cook for Rose. She told Rose that she was to eat only the food that I prepared for her, and that the only things she had to give up were meat and coffee. Rose made a slight face at this, as she really loved her meat and her one cup of coffee in the morning. I eventually broke down to her pleadings and gave her about a third of a cup a day.

She told Rose that the one goodie that she could have was yogurt, the kind sold in the health food stores. Besides the different fruit that came with them, which made them quite tasty, they contained live Acidophilus. She then added that inside all people's intestines lived bacteria _ it was divided between good and bad bacteria. When the body was healthy, they kept each other in check. When a person was given anti-biotics, be it older people or young children, the anti-biotics killed the good bacteria. They spread into the urinary tract, and every other place that they could. That's what Rose had been complaining to the doctors about for quite some time. She had a very bad urinary infection. They had no drugs capable of clearing up the infection, so Rose was left to suffer with it, for I don't know how long a time. The doctor explained that the live acidophilus from the yogurt attack the bad bacteria and eventually Rose's infection would be cleared up.

Dr. G had a list of all the things that Rose was to take and started to explain it to me. Every once in a while the girls would break in with a question, which the doctor would answer before continuing her instructions to me.

When she was all done, she showed me a bill with

the list of things she had brought and she said she was going to add on twenty dollars for the cost of the visit. When it looked at the bill and it only came to two-hundred and thirty-six dollars, I was stunned. Once I went to a naturopathic doctor in Anchorage for an allergy that we figured out after the third visit was an allergic reaction to my changing my brand of soap. For the first visit of any new patient, his fee was one hundred and eighty dollars. The cost of each visit dropped down to eighty dollars for each visit after that. I went to him because he was the most famous naturopath in Alaska, and he turned out to be one of the nicest people that I have ever met. In all of my dealings with people in the health business, from doctors to the clerks and owners of health food stores, they all fit into the same pattern of caring and helpfulness. I didn't mind paying his bill one bit.

Then Rose asked the doctor if she was permitted to keep taking her drugs. I didn't realize at the time how vital this question was. Dr. G hesitated for a while and then said, "It's up to you, Rose." I took her literally and continued to give Rose her drugs whenever she asked for them.

I proceeded to clean out Rose's refrigerator because, with all of the junk food she had there, there wasn't enough room for all the food that I purchased. I threw out over two dozen doughnuts, several quarts of ice cream, and a couple pieces of layer cake. There were some TV dinners in there that featured hamburger steak. All this and more I threw into the garbage before there was enough room for all the food that I had bought.

I bought a steamer like the one I had back in Anchorage. In it I steamed her vegetables, chicken, and fish. She enjoyed this as they came out so nice and tender. I made beans and rice, sweet potatoes, and pasta, too. She continued to get her Meals on Wheels and, when it would arrive, I would put it on the table and look at it. After opening it, I might decide that we could keep some little bit of the salad if it wasn't wilted. Rose would look at the ham, or whatever the meat was that day, with deep longing. Although she missed eating that crap, she didn't say a word as I threw it out.

The dieticians that plan these meals, as well as the ones that plan the meals for hospitals, have no idea what proper food combining is, and the people that eat these meals for any length of time usually wind up suffering from malnutrition and indigestion on top of their other woes.

The supplements and other things that Dr. G brought, plus the food that Rose was now eating, were designed to cure malnutrition.

My days then fell into a routine that I followed for the next 25 of them. In the morning I would make breakfast and then wash the dishes. Then I would give Rose the drugs she took for her Parkinsons. Then into a shaker I would put one level teaspoon of All-One, one level teaspoon of calcium citrate (calcium in powder form), and some apple juice. After mixing it thoroughly, I would pour it into a large glass that had a straw in it. Rose found it easier to drink all of her liquids that way. Along with that, I gave her one chrome pill, one lecithin pill, one thymus pill, and two garlic pills. A little later I would put one teaspoon of Kyogreen in a glass of water, stir and give it to Rose. Along with the Kyo, I have her one thyroid pill, one adrenal pill, one Vitamin E pill, and one CO Q 10 pill.

Soon after this she would ask for her pain pills. She had Xanax, which she sometimes combined with a Tylenol. She had other brands of pain pills that I gave her when she asked for them.

I would then give her a tablespoon of Dr.

Thurston's K. It contained potassium and magnesium, which was good for energy and which I later found out tasted good. In between I made some carrot juice for both of us to drink.

If she was having protein in her lunch that day, I would also give her some cottage cheese with one tablespoon of flaxseed oil stirred into it. If it was a starch meal that day, I would give it to her early enough so that it would be digested before the starch entered her stomach. With her lunch I gave her cranberry juice to drink to help correct her kidney problems. After lunch I would give her a digestive enzyme pill, one lecithin pill, one chrome pill, and two garlic pills.

After that I would go shopping and then go spend some time with my sisters, Ann or Kay, who lived close by. I would also occasionally make the long trip to Green Tree, which was just past Pittsburgh, where Martha lives. Some of the days I would just jump into bed for a nap. I wasn't getting too much sleep at night, so I tried to make up for it whenever I could

After fixing dinner and washing the dishes, I gave Rose one digestive enzyme pill, one chrome pill, one CO Q 10, along with her drink of Kyogreen. Then another tablespoon of Dr. Thurston's. The last thing that I gave her was a powdered form of Bio Oxygen in a glass of water, followed by a teaspoon of powdered Vitamin C in another glass of water. I used distilled water which I purchased at the local grocery store for all our drinking needs.

After giving Rose some more of her drugs, I would lay on the couch and watch a basketball game or some other program. Most of the time I would fall asleep as I lay there.

When Rose was ready for bed, I would go back with her, give her a sleeping pill, and help her into bed.

Then I would go to sleep myself. Then the cycle would start over again.

During the course of the day, Rose would get up from her reclining chair for a trip to the bathroom. She did this quite often. In the mornings she would move at a fairly steady pace, but as the day wore on she shuffled slower and slower going down the hall to the bathroom.

Slowly but surely a horrible suspicion began to enter my mind. I remembered last year on my trip home when one day I noticed she had trouble stretching her arms. I said to her, "Your arthritis in your neck must be awful bad and painful because you can hardly move your arms." She answered that, yes, it was terrible. I tried to get her to move her arms in some stretching exercises, but she couldn't do them.

Rather than try to work the arthritis out of her neck because it hurt when she moved, she quit moving her upper body. Her whole upper body was starting to atrophy.

I also remembered back to the year before when, on my visit home, my family had thrown a surprise party for me on my sixty-fifth birthday. It was a very nice party and it was wonderful having all the sisters and so many nieces and nephews running around. I wandered into the kitchen where I found Rose complaining to several of her daughters of her pain. I guess they had gotten tired of her always talking about it, for one of them said, "Christ, take a tranquilizer, take two of them!"

I asked Rose if she was sure she had Parkinsons. She said, yes, she had gone to several doctors about it. She said that the first doctor had attached some kind of wires to her upper arms. They were attached to a machine that gave him a reading. He said, "You don't have any muscle tone in your arms. You, therefore, have Parkinsons." He then prescribed some drugs for her. She said that when she walked into the second doctor's office, the first thing he said to her was, "What are you here for?" When she told him she was there for a second opinion on her Parkinsons diagnosis, he said, "Oh, yeah?" Then he gave her a very brief examination, after which he told her, "Yes, you have Parkinsons," and gave her more drugs to take for it.

I said, "Rose, didn't they say anything about your lack of palsy? People with Parkinsons are supposed to have palsy and their hands are supposed to be shaking all the time." To myself I thought about the only time I had seen her hand shake. It was one day when one of her daughters had brought over some documents for her to fill out. While Rose was filling them out, her hands were jerking all over the place. It was only later that I realized that Rose did this so her family wouldn't question their not shaking.

I then said, "Rose, I don't think you have Parkinsons. I think that by not moving your upper body, it has started to atrophy. When that happened, you lost all of your muscle tone. When the doctor's machine showed no muscle tone, that's when he said you had Parkinsons." I continued by saying that she was misdiagnosed and was taking medication for something that she didn't have. She said, "You're no doctor. I believe those doctors." I didn't say anything about it from then on.

I think that Rose was happy when those doctors told her she had Parkinsons, and that she wore that Parkinsons label like a medal so that she could say to her kids, "There, I told you I was sick."

One morning I had gotten up quite early and was sitting in the living room reading the paper. I looked up and there came Rose walking down the hall. She didn't have her stroller and she walked as if there was nothing wrong with her. She did something in the kitchen then she turned and walked briskly back down the hall and into her room. She then went into the bathroom where she took a shower all by herself. While she was there, I almost did a cartwheel I was so happy. I thought to myself that the medicine supplements and good food must have finally kicked in and she was now getting better. I said, "Thank you, Lord, Allah, Odin, and all the rest of you guys."

After her shower, she put on some nice clothes instead of the housecoat that she usually wore. After she sat in her reclining chair I asked her about her remarkable performance that morning. She said, "I don't know what came over me. I just felt like doing all those things." After a little more talk on how good she felt and that she was now over the hump and on the road to recovery, we settled into our usual routine.

As the day wore on, and as I kept giving Rose more of her drugs, I noticed one thing. On her trips to the bathroom Rose's movements got slower and slower with each trip. By the time she was ready to go to bed for the night, she was back down to a slow shuffle.

After Rose went to bed, I went looking for something. I don't remember what it was right now, but when I looked into a drawer of one of her dressers I found something that made everything perfectly clear to me. In Pennsylvania the druggist has to give you a printout of the contents of each drug and their side effects. In the drawer I found a folder filled with a bunch of those printouts. When I left Roses, I took some of the printouts, but not all of them. Here is a list of some of those drugs I found and their side effects:

Carbidopa and Levodopa: To treat Parkinsons
Side effects: Stomach upset, loss of appetite, dry mouth, change in taste, headache or dizziness. CHECK WITH YOUR DOCTOR if you experience vomiting,

severe abdominal pain, unusual or painful movements of face, diarrhea, depression, or confusion.

Bethanchol: To treat urinary infection
Side effects: Dizziness, stomachache, irregular heartbeat, sweating, and breathing problems.

Doxazosin: To treat benign prostatic hyperplasia
Side effects: Dizziness, headache, nausea, drowsiness, lack of energy, dry mouth, or nasal congestion.

Nabumetone: To relieve pain and swelling
Side effects: Stomach upset, drowsiness, easy bruising, reports of trouble breathing, bloody stools, bad stomach pains. Avoid alcohol and aspirin while taking this drug.

Propoxyphene with Acetaminophen: To relieve pain
Side effects: Drowsiness, dizziness, constipation, nausea or vomiting. Report jaundice, rash, or hives to doctor.

Stool softener/combination laxative: To treat constipation
Side effects: Gas, bloating, or rectal irritation may occur. Notify your doctor of nausea, vomiting, rectal bleeding, or chest pains.

Meclizine/Buclizine/cycl: To prevent/treat nausea, vomiting, or dizziness
Side effects: Thirst, dry mouth, or drowsiness. Report mental change, rash, rapid heartbeat, or difficult urination.

Ciprofloxacin: This medicine is used to treat infections. Cautions: This medicine may cause increased sensitivity to the sun. If you plan on becoming pregnant, discuss with our doctor the benefits and risks of using this medicine.
Side effects: Nausea, vomiting, loss of appetite,

dizziness, headache, nervousness, or trouble sleeping. Check with your doctor if you experience: Rash, swelling of throat or tongue, difficulty breathing, itching, or hives.

Bromocriptine: To treat a hormonal or nervous system problem

Side effects: Bloody stool, confusion, weakness, persistent runny nose, vomiting, drowsiness.

Trazodone: To treat nervousness

Side effects: Drowsiness, report of dizziness, fainting, blood in urine, heart problems, breathing problems.

I did not have any printout on Xanax, nor did I know what the combination of Xanax and Tylenol would cause, but I assumed it wouldn't be very good. As you go down the list, you can see how the side effect of one drug would cause the taking of another drug to try to correct. That would cause a call for another drug, and so on down the line.

The next morning I confronted Rose with these reports. She sat there as I read off all of the side effects to her. After I was done reading them, she said, "The doctor said I have to take all this stuff and I'm not going to change. After all, he is a doctor and he knows what he is talking about."

We then continued with the old routine, with me constantly preaching to her the evils of the drugs she was taking. I told her heavy drug users eventually died from peptic ulcers and from holes in the colon made by drugs that let poisons seep back into the body.

A few nights later, I heard the tinkle of her bell and went in and helped her out of bed. She started walking to the bathroom without her walker. After a few steps, her feet stumbled and she headed for the floor, head first. After I got her back to her feet, she thought that she was seriously hurt and called an ambulance to take her to the hospital.

When the ambulance came, the two fellows tied Rose on to a stretcher and carried her out to the ambulance. They then came in and asked for a list of all her medication. I guess this falling from the effects of the drugs was a common occurrence, and they acted in a practiced routine.

In a few days one of Rose's daughters brought her home from the hospital. I guess Rose must have told them that I was trying to cut down on her drugs. As soon as they got her seated in her chair they asked her what drugs she wanted. They then went to the drugs and got what she had requested. I started to tell them that the drugs were the major part of Rose's problem, but they were already prepared for this statement. They said, "Well, that Dr. G didn't tell her to stop taking them, did she?" I kept my mouth shut the rest of the time that they were there. In a short while they left and there I was once again with Rose.

I started to go about the old routine but I couldn't stand it. I had to once again talk to Rose about what those drugs would do to her. I said, "Rose, you know that all of your daughters are married and have husbands, children, and jobs that they are busy with. They don't have time to come over and take care of you." I told her she should try to quit those drugs and to let me get on with the supplements and proper diet so that she could improve enough to take care of herself. I told her that if she didn't do that one of these days she was going to find herself laying in her own piss and shit in some nursing home praying for one of the attendants to come and change her. Nothing I said did any good. She kept saying that the doctors knew what they were doing. I told her if she didn't try to quit the drugs that I was going to leave. She said,

"That's up to you."

I went into my room and packed my clothes. I took the juicer out to the car. When I came back I told her that I was going to leave the supplements for her. She said, "No, take them. I'm too weak to take them myself. I can hardly lift my hands."

As I drove the fifteen miles to Martha's house, it's a wonder that I didn't wreck the car. I cried all the way there with the thought in my mind of what the future held in store for Rose. When I got to Martha's, I phoned Rose. I told her that if she changed her mind and tried to quit the drugs I would come back and try to help her again. She said she would think about it and hung up.

For the next few days I did nothing but eat and sleep at Martha's as I was exhausted, both mentally and physically. Martha was very understanding and cooked me some nice meals and let me recuperate.

On the third day Rose called. I guess she missed all of the tender loving care I had given her, and possibly the loneliness and realization that what I had been talking about might come true. She said that she realized that the drugs weren't helping her and was ready to try it my way.

The next day I drove to Rose's. On the way in I was singing and happy as I thought that maybe now we can get to work in earnest. After I did all of the morning half of my routine, I told Rose that I was going shopping and maybe I would take sister Ann out to lunch. I started to pack up the drugs to take with me. Rose said, "Why don't you just leave them in their usual place?" I said, "No way!" I was getting a little smarter and took all of the drugs with me.

I went shopping and then went and picked Ann up. We had a very nice lunch, over which we talked of old times. I reminded her of all the times that brother Dan and I had asked her to cook roast pork for our Sunday dinner. She put a lot of garlic into it and she had the cooking time down perfectly. It always turned out so good that we gorged ourselves. As we lay on couches in the living room, too stuffed to move, Ann, fishing for a compliment, would ask, "How was it?" We always answered in unison, "We ate it, didn't we?"

After about four hours I returned to Rose's. She acted as if she were possessed, pleading with me for some of her drugs. In fifteen years of driving a cab, I have driven a lot of drug addicts around. Addicts are everywhere and I could tell that they were looking for drugs as I drove them from house to house. They would be twitching and jerky as we drove around looking. But I could tell when they came out of a house happy and smiling and floating on cloud nine that they had found their magic dream giver. Rose was acting the same way and I realized that there was nothing that I could do for her. The drugs had her really hooked and the only way she could quit them was to go into some special rehabilitation sanitarium that knew how to cure her.

I gave Rose some of the drug she requested and then told her that I was leaving once again. I told her that there was nothing I could do for her and that I was leaving for Anchorage in a short time.

I moved back into Martha's place for a few days. I called the airlines and had my ticket changed so that I could get out of there as soon as possible. The combination of my failure with Rose and the extreme humidity made me want to get right back to Alaska.

As I sat on that plane going home, I remembered reading a report, stating some very high figure, of how many people died as a result of their drug use. I tried to imagine how many other people there were who, just like

Rose, were sitting in their lonely apartments or houses waiting for the next drug that came on the market. Waiting for that special magic drug that the drug companies always promised would transport them back to perfect health and a relief from their suffering. After reading of the billions and billions of dollars that the drug companies were spending to buy each other out, it was easy to surmise that the figure was in the millions. The drug companies have their teeth chomped down on the teat of a golden cow that spits out hundred dollar bills, and there is no way that they are going to let go.

I arrived back in Anchorage very sad and dejected. I went back to work, but it took several months for me to get rid of my depression.

Rose was admitted to a nursing home a little after I left Pittsburgh.

1990
My Lung Cancer Scare

One day I was at the clinic seeing my favorite doctor, Dr. S. I don't remember the reason for my being there. It may have been for a physical or some other minor ailment. Whenever something on me wasn't up to snuff, I would immediately go down to see the doctor. A lot of people don't go to the doctor right away because they are afraid to hear bad news. I knew that the sooner, the better, and the doctor would heal me.

The doctor said to me, "I see you smoke. How many cigarettes a day do you smoke?" When I told him between two and three packs a day, he said that I should have my chest x-rayed. He told me that if they saw a circle about as big as a quarter, that was cancer and they couldn't do anything about it.

After they took the pictures, they hung them up on the wall so that you could look at them. I could swear that I saw a quarter-sized circle in the picture. The nurse came into the room and told me that the doctor was busy with other patients and wouldn't be able to see me that day. She said that they had to send the pictures to another lab to be evaluated and to call their office in seven to ten days to find out the results.

I went home convinced that I had lung cancer and didn't have too much longer to live. I threw my cigarettes away and quit smoking. Of course, that was like locking the barn after all the horses ran away. I called the mortuary up and found out that it costs seven hundred and fifty dollars to get cremated. At night I would lay in bed and pray to the gods to please let me live. I made them a lot of promises, if they would only let me live. I thought back to all the times that I had said, when somebody had mentioned my smoking, "when it's my turn, I'll go." I found out that when the chips were down and when I thought I was dying, I didn't want to go.

Waiting that seven days to call and find out the results was like waiting seven months. Each day passed ever so slowly. Finally on the seventh day, I called. When the phone rang, I braced myself, waiting to hear the bad news. I gave my name to the nurse who answered the phone and waited all aquiver for the results. She came back on the phone and casually said, "you're okay, everything's fine." What a relief.

I was so happy that I went up to the local bar to celebrate. Of course, it goes without saying that after quite a few beers, I reached for a cigarette. Sorry, gods.

The next time I went in, I got a woman doctor. After she got done with my exam, she said, "I see you smoke. Since you're here, why don't we take some x-rays of your lungs?" I asked her how much it would cost. She said eighty dollars. I then said, "If they find cancer, what could you do for me?" She said, "Nothing, just let you know that you are dying." I said, "Thanks, but no thanks."

I finally did quit smoking about five years ago. It happened about the time I started turning into a health nut.

All of the smoking that I had done started to constrict my blood vessels. My feet were starting to get cold and my thighs were aching. In other words, I wasn't getting any circulation in my legs. I would quit smoking for a week and my feet would start to tingle. That was a sign that my blood vessels were dilating and that I was once again getting circulation. The pain would go away, and I would feel a lot better. Of course, when the pain went away, that called for another smoke, and the cycle would start over again.

Finally the pain got so bad that I just had to quit. I could hardly walk, and the pain in my legs was unbearable. I threw the pack away and haven't smoked since.

I bought a machine similar to a Nordic Track. It was just like skiing. The first time I tried it, I lasted for about two minutes. I got off and I was panting and puffing like a locomotive going up a real steep incline. I stuck it out, and every day stayed on it longer and longer, until I built my lungs back up. In no time at all, I got to where I could keep going for twenty and thirty minutes at a time.

1990
My Barium Enema

I got a job as a cab driver. I only took it as a part-time job. I was a construction worker. I installed acoustical ceilings. That was my occupation for over twenty years. I really enjoyed it, and it was an active job — always on the go, climbing scaffolds and ladders all day.

I only took the cab job as a fill-in job because the construction business was slow and I got tired of laying around the house all day.

When I got a call to go back to installing suspended ceilings, I declined because I had gotten to like cab driving. I enjoyed meeting people from all walks of life, and I enjoyed talking to them as I took them to their destinations.

I used to read both of our daily papers every day so that I was up on most everything that was happening in the world. People would tell me what their occupation was and then would be really surprised when I started talking about some issue that was related to their work. It made quite a difference from the construction industry, where there wasn't anyone to talk to for most of the day, as I usually worked in a room all by myself. This way, I had a captive audience.

I used to smoke two to three packs of cigarettes a day. Over the years I tried so many different times to quit smoking. I used to throw my cigarettes out of the window of my cab and swear never again, but it never worked.

One of the times that I tried to quit smoking, I decided that every time I wanted a cigarette, I would chew some non-fat chewing gum instead. I was chewing two to three boxes of sugarless gum every day. The only trouble with that is that I was chewing constantly, and the gum was sweetened with something called Sorbitol.

In a very short time I started going to the bathroom quite frequently. In fact, I developed diarrhea. I was also seeing blood on the toilet paper after I wiped. It finally dawned on me that the Sorbitol in the chewing gum was the culprit. I immediately stopped chewing the gum, and my diarrhea quit.

Some time after this, I was down to the clinic to take a physical that was required by the Department of Motor Vehicles. Just as we were getting finished, I casually mentioned to Dr. S. about the blood I had been passing. I told him that it had stopped after I quit chewing the gum and that everything was now okay. He told me that when there is blood like that, I should have my colon checked, in case there was cancer. He told me that there were two procedures that they used. One was a sigmoidoscopy, and the other was a barium enema. He told me that both procedures would cost a total of about four hundred and fifty dollars. I told him that I could handle that, and so we went ahead and made an appointment.

I took the sigmoidoscopy in the doctor's office. He had me lay down on a table and proceeded to put a long, thin instrument up my anus. There was a light on the end of it, and he could see the inside of my lower colon. After he pulled it back out, he told me that he didn't see anything in my colon, but he did notice that my hemorrhoids were inflamed. I reminded him about what I had said about the gum, but it didn't get any response.

A short time later I had an appointment at the hospital for a barium enema. The night before the appointment, I had to take a very powerful laxative to get my colon cleaned out.

I had never had an enema before, so I was very

tense when I laid down on the table to receive it. To my surprise, it was very simple, with no pain or discomfort. I guess the liquid that they put into me made it easier to take x-rays of my colon.

I laid on that table for fifteen or twenty minutes with that liquid inside of me, until they took all of the pictures that they needed. The technician then had me go into the bathroom and expel the water. Was sure surprised at how easy it all was.

About a week later Dr. S. called and said that I didn't have anything to worry about as they didn't find anything.

I know Dr. S. was only worried about my health when he insisted on these tests, but if he would have listened to me about the chewing gum I could have saved that four hundred and fifty dollars.

But to me it was worth it as it introduced me to the Enema and I was very thankful for that instant compatibility. See next chapter on Enemas.

The Enema Bag

Being single and having never learned to cook, my
diet was terrible. I used to eat a lot of sandwiches made of
bologna or ham on white bread. Or in the course of a
twelve-hour shift of driving my cab, I would eat two or
three doughnuts. When I say doughnuts, I mean those
great big ones called apple fritters. As a consequence of
this, I was constantly constipated. By eating like this, I
really suffered. I used to drive around in my cab feeling
really tired and sluggish from my constipation. After a
couple of days of a bloated stomach and that dragging
feeling, I would head for my Ex-Lax bottle. The only way I
could get my bowels to move would be to take two of the
Ex-Lax pills instead of one. The next day, I would go to
the bathroom two or three times, and it was really
miserable. Taking them two or three times a week was
really rough on my body. I used to take so many Ex-Lax
pills that I always thought that I should buy stock in the
company to get some of my money back.

Like most people, when you mention an enema, I
used to wrinkle up my nose and say, "no enema for me."
But after my barium enema and seeing how easy it was,
you could say it was instant love between me and that bag.
No more sitting on that darn toilet waiting for the coffee to
kick in and make me go or taking any more Ex-Lax.

In all of the articles I have read, they all stress
enemas and keeping the colon clean, so I guess I do owe
Dr. S. a vote of thanks for getting me started on them.

The books all say that you should take an enema
every day with cancer and at least once a week without it,
to keep your colon clean.

I usually put the juice of one-half lemon into the

bag, fill it up with warm water, and then put a clothes hanger through the bottom and hang it on the end of the shower curtain. I apply a little bit of olive oil to my anus and then insert the end of the tube.

I had read somewhere that coffee enemas were very good for the liver, as they clean out the bile and toxins that accumulate there. Not knowing any better, I proceeded to make a normal pot of coffee of six cups. I put all six cups into my bag, and then into me. I laid down and held it in for about 15 minutes. There was a lot of bile that came out, but I had a coffee high that was out of this world. I guess all that caffeine worked its way into my bloodstream and all through my body. I had to go to bed and just lay there for hours, with my eyes refusing to close.

I have since learned that you are supposed to just use one cup of coffee, diluted with one cup of water. After you insert the coffee, lay on the bed and switch from laying on your right side to your back and then to your left side. After fifteen minutes, head for the bathroom and expel it.

1991-1996
Hair Growth

In my youth I was blessed with a thick mop of
blond hair. It was so thick that it was a struggle pulling a
comb through it. With the fire that singed some of it out,
that I describe under *Juicing*, and the advancement of my
years, it came down to where I was very thin on top. One
time I decided that by rubbing Vitamin E into my scalp I
could stimulate the scalp enough to grow new hair. I
talked my buddy, Fred, into the notion and soon we were
both breaking open capsules of Vitamin E and rubbing it
into our scalps. Needless to say, no new hair.

Another time, while I was at the airport reading my
scandal sheets I came across an article about olive oil. It
seems that this fellow came into a doctor's office with a rash
on his head. The doctor told him to put some olive oil on
it. A short time later, the patient returned to the doctor's
office. Not only was the rash gone but he was growing a
lot of new hair. The story then went on to talk about the
Italians. It told of how all Italians used so much olive oil in
their everyday life and that this accounted for the thick,
lustrous hair that they all had.

Now I had forgotten that most of the stories
written in two of the scandal sheets were written by people
that had imaginations that originated in outer space
somewhere. I usually bought these for the laughs they
provided. They are the *News* and the *Sun*. Once I had
read an article in one of them that said *WD-40*, the spray
that mechanics use on rusty bolts and nuts, was good for
arthritis. It claimed that a bunch of people put it on their
arthritic joints and it reduced their pain very much. I was
going around telling my sister Martha and everybody about

it for a while, before I realized that it was a sham. Maybe because I wanted to believe the article so much, I forgot where I read it.

I told my buddy Fred about it and soon we were both putting the olive oil on our heads. I walked around with an oily, greasy scalp for quite a while before I realized that it was another sham.

One day I was in the health food store to buy some vitamins. As I stood by one of the shelves trying to decide which brand of vitamin to buy, one of the salesgirls came over and started to stock a shelf right next to me. I jokingly asked her if she had anything in the store to grow hair. She picked up a bottle from the shelf and handed it to me. The bottle was labeled with the name Recidivil. On the back of the bottle it read that it was distributed by Strata Dermatologics, Concord, CA 94518. The directions on the bottle said to apply one half dropper full of Recidivil to the scalp twice daily. I purchased two bottles and went looking for Fred. I told him that our search was over. He said, "Not this time. You come and show me some new hair before I fall for any more of your pipedreams."

I started using it and in a short time new hair started to grow. I hurried to tell Fred the good news. After seeing the new hair growing on my head, he told me he was going to go to the health flood store and pick some up.

After my two bottles ran out, I returned to the health food store to buy some more. They had run out and had some on order. I think Fred got the last two bottles. I went to another health food store to see if they carried Recidivil. They didn't, but the girl there talked me into using an oil based product that they sold. You were supposed to heat a little up and then massage your scalp with it.

I bought a bottle, went home, and started using it.

After about the fourth day of putting that oil on my head I took a real good look at my hair in the mirror. The oil had burned a lot of my new hair out. There were real tears in my eyes as I poured that bottle of oil down the sink.

I was sitting in my cab parked at the Bush Company waiting for a fare to come out when Mike, my buddy who was parked in back of me, came up and sat in my cab.

I told him about the bad luck I had with my hair, and he told me that I should try a product that he was using that was really working for him. He raved about it so much I asked him for the telephone number of the company that made it so that I could order some.

When my order (which cost one-hundred sixty dollars) came in it consisted of two different treatments. One of the bottles had some herbs in a shampoo like mixture that you put on your hair and leave it on for five minutes before you rinse it out.

The second bottle you put on after your shower. You put it on and then brush your head for 10 minutes on each side.

The literature in the box it came in said that they had developed a special brush to use. If they had mentioned that on the phone when I placed my order, I would gladly have spent the extra money to buy their brush, but since I didn't want to wait the two weeks or so that I would have to wait for the brush to come through the mail, I decided to just go over to Wal-Mart and buy a brush.

At Wal-Mart they had over a hundred different brushes hanging on their display rack. After looking at five or six brushes I randomly took one.

The bristles on the brush were very hard but since I had never used a hairbrush I just assumed all of the brushes were like that.

After several days of using the brush I took a good look in the mirror and realized that the brush had pulled out a lot of my new hair.

I stepped out on the balcony of my apartment and threw that brush as far as I could throw it.

I went back to the first health food store. Their back order had come in and I bought two bottles of the Recidivil. But now, instead of putting a half dropper of it on my hair twice a day, I use a full dropper twice a day. I check my head very carefully every day and I think new hair is still coming in. Even though I lost most of my new hair because of that oil and brush, as I look into the mirror the new hair that is still there looks like a small forest to me.

Fred is very pleased with the Recidivil. His hair is growing, too, and he is happy that we finally hit on a product that worked.

I read in the papers that the drug companies were going to put Rogaine into the drug stores. They said that it grows hair and that you wouldn't need a prescription to buy it. I wouldn't care if it grew so much hair on my head that I would have to use a lawn mower to cut it, I still wouldn't use it. With all of the side affects associated with drugs, it would be just my luck that some of it would settle into my head and damage my brain.

If your hair is a drab gray or even has a touch of yellow in it, here's what to do. Get some Johnson's Baby Oil and rub it into your hair. Your hair will turn a beautiful silver-gray.

I have found out that there is one bet you can make and win money. The bet is about bald men. If you see a man who is pretty bald with even just a little fringe around the sides, bet whoever you are with that fellow that has a comb in his pocket. Most bald men are jolly and won't hit you and will show you their comb.

Hair One Year Later

One year later I was down in Seattle on vacation visiting old friends. I stopped into a health food store to pick up some Kyogreen as my supply was getting dangerously low, and I hated to go a day without my morning energy giver.

As I walked the aisles browsing, a white tube caught my eye. The name on it was Polysorbate 80, with Biotin and Niacin. Now, I knew that my Recidivil had biotin in it so that's why I picked it up.

On the back it said to put a thin coat over the scalp and balding areas, rub until head is slightly warm, and then shower. It made no claims that it would grow hair but I surmised that it would, so I bought it.

The next day I moved into the home of Ed Brown, a very good friend for many years. He and his wife, Charmaine, have a very nice home in Tacoma, Washington and I really enjoyed my visit with them.

On the last day there I told Charmaine that my scalp was really itching me and asked if she would take a took at it. She did and she said she saw a lot of little black spots on my head and couldn't figure out what they were. I excitedly told her that it was new hair growing.

When I got back to Anchorage, I picked up the phone and when he answered said, "Hey Fred, guess what?"

1991
My Prostate and Essiac Tea
Cancer Cure

I had always read and heard advertised that when you get older, you should see a urologist to check your prostate. Since I started having trouble urinating, I thought that I should follow that advice.

Most people would ask their friends or other people to recommend a good doctor. Don't do like I did. I looked in the Yellow Pages under "Urologists." There were quite a few listed. I came to the name, Dr. R, and said to myself, "there's a good German name, he must be pretty good."

I made an appointment and the doctor seemed very nice. I told him that I has having trouble urinating and that I got up two or three times a night to go to the bathroom.

He gave me some paper cups to take home with me to check my flow of urine. When I next saw the doctor, he told me that he wanted to look up inside my bladder. He also had me get a physical from a regular doctor.

The day of the bladder examination, he gave me a shot that numbed the lower part of my body. I just laid there while he stuck a tube into my penis. The tube had a light on the end of it and he just looked around inside my bladder.

A week later, I was back at the doctor's office. He told me that he didn't see any cancer in my bladder but that he wanted to take my prostate out. He said that he would schedule me into the hospital in two weeks and that I was to see him one day before the operation.

Needless to say, when I left the doctor's office, I

was in a state of shock. I decided that I had better find out a little bit more about the prostate. I went to a First Care clinic. A First Care clinic is one that you go to for minor emergencies. I met a very nice doctor there. He didn't have any of my paperwork and had nothing to go on except what I told him. He explained everything about the prostate and then told me that usually they don't take out the prostate, but just ream it out to let the urine flow easier.

The day before my scheduled operation, I was back to Dr. R's office. I told him what the other doctor said and that I didn't want the operation. I told him that I was going to see another urologist to get a second opinion. He said, no, no, no. He said that he was just going to ream it out. When he said that, I said okay.

The next day he proceeded with the operation. I had a catheter for the first two days after the operation. When they took it out, they told me to drink plenty of water, which I did. About six hours later, after having not gone to the bathroom and my stomach started to bulge out, I though it was about time to mention it to the nurse. She immediately got a tube which she put up into my penis and got my urine to flow. What a relief. After three days, I went home.

When I got home, I guess I must have contracted an infection in my urinary tract. I called the doctor up and told him about it, and he called a prescription into the drug store for me. After a week of taking the sulfa pills that he prescribed for me, there was no let-up from the pain every time I urinated.

I went over and mentioned the problem to the druggist. He recommended a salve for me to squeeze into my penis. I called the doctor and told him of the druggist's recommendation, and he called the druggist and gave his okay. What a blessed relief it was to finally urinate without the burning pain. Two weeks later I went back to work driving my cab.

About two weeks after that, the doctor's office called me up. They wanted me to come in to see the doctor. When I arrived, he told me that when he sent the tissue into some main lab for analysis, they found a little bit of cancer. He said that he wanted to ream me out some more to make sure he got everything, and I readily agreed.

The second operation went very smoothly. No complications and not too much pain, so I went home in two days.

I was just about ready to go back to Pennsylvania for a vacation with my family when I got another call from the doctor's office. The doctor told me that he wanted to do another operation. He said he was going back into the army and he wanted to take my prostate out before he went. He said that if I didn't have the operation, I would die of cancer. The side effects of the operation were impotency and no control of urination.

I asked him how much longer would I live without the operation. He said, "I don't know, I'm not God."

Needless to say, my visit was a very sad one. I spent a few days at each of my four sisters' houses, and the last day at the home of my niece, Eileen Kerr. I was saying good-bye to everyone, and I was also looking for a copy of the book, *Final Exit*. It was a book advertised on how to commit suicide. Eileen asked if I wanted to stay with her for my last days, as I was convinced that the end was near. I didn't want to be a burden, so thanked her very much, but declined.

The day before I was due to go back to Alaska, I said to Eileen, "Gee, I wish I knew more about the prostate." She said that she had a big medical book and brought it out. Under prostate cancer, the first sentence was, "Men in their sixties who develop prostate cancer will probably die of some other ailment before they die of cancer." This is because it grows so slowly and it takes many years before it is life threatening. What a relief.

When I got back to Anchorage, I went to the doctor's office. When I told him about reading about how long it takes for prostate to kill you, he said, "Oh, yes, it takes a long time to grow." I don't know why I didn't beat the hell out of him right then. I regret it to this day. He was just a small, skinny jerk, and I was probably afraid that I would kill him if I started to beat him.

As I mentioned earlier, I do a lot of reading. In the cab business, you have a lot of time to sit around waiting for fares. In addition to our two daily papers that we had at the time, I read all of the scandal sheets every week. I never missed the Enquirer, the Star, the Sun and every other one they put out. They helped to pass the time, and you get a lot of health tips out of them. Just before I went to Pittsburgh, I saw an ad in one of them that read, "Send forty dollars and we will send you a book that tells all about the prostate." The book arrived and it said to check if you have prostate cancer, get a PSA blood test.

I went down to the local VA clinic and explained my situation to Dr. F. He said, "I know Dr. R, he's a good man. You should go ahead and have the operation, as you would have about twenty more years of life." I said, "No, just give me this PSA test."

A week or so later, I went down for the results of the PSA test. The doctor wasn't in the clinic that day so they had a nurse take care of me. She opened the file where I could look at it and explained it to me. She said "the prostate gives off these things called antigens. When it is normal, the reading is 4.0. When there is cancer, the reading goes up. Your reading is 0.5. You are in wonderful shape."

I know there are a lot of good doctors, but why did I pick the bad one.

I wrote a letter to the Editor and it appeared in our daily paper. I wanted to alert all of Dr. R's patients about him. I mentioned that people should always get a second opinion.

A little later, I found out that I didn't even need the operation. The doctors have something called Proscar. I think that is the name of it. The only trouble is that there are side effects with it. At the health food store you can pick up some Saw Palmeto. It shrinks the prostate with no side effects.

On my next trip to Pittsburgh, at the East End Food Co-op, I saw a book on the rack that caught my eye. The title of the book was *The Essiac Report, Canada's Remarkable Unknown Cancer Remedy*[1]. I was so caught up in the story that I hardly put it down until I finished reading it. When I was done with it, I was a believer.

Essiac is named after the name of the nurse Caisse who invented it. It is her name spelled backwards.

I didn't know if our health food stores carried any in Anchorage, so I stopped at the East End Food Co-op in Pittsburgh to stock up on it. There was quite a line at the check-out counter, and as I waited in line, the fellow in back of me tapped on my shoulder to get my attention. When I turned around, he said, "I notice you have a lot of Essiac tea in your cart. Do you want to know what it did for me?"

When I said yes, he said that it cured his prostate cancer. He said his reading had been really high, but it was now down to 2.5.

A few weeks after returning to Anchorage, I received a telephone call from my niece Eileen. She told me that a very close friend of her husband George had prostate cancer and asked if I had any suggestions. She said his reading was 248. I told her that he should try the Essiac tea. A few weeks later she called to tell me that his PSA reading was now 1.4 and they said, "Thank God for Essiac tea."

I recently went down to California to visit an old boyhood buddy of mine, Al N. We had grown up together, but I hadn't seen him in many years.

After a few hours of reminiscing about old times, the conversation turned to health. Al said that when we were young all the conversations were about sex, but now that we are old, all we talk about is our health.

He then said that he was having a miserable time with his prostate. It was swollen up and even though he used the doctor's medicine and saw palmetto, it wouldn't go down. He was an avid bowler and the pressure put on his prostate when he bent down to bowl made him pass a lot of blood when he urinated.

After quite a bit of friendly persuasion I got him to try Essiac tea. After about two weeks the bleeding stopped. I told him that the tea must have shrunk his prostate. I have talked to him a few times on the phone since returning to Anchorage, and he has told me that all of his troubles are over.

They say that once cancer is cut into, some of it gets into your blood stream and it travels to different parts of your body. Then it will eventually show up. Even though my PSA blood test of 0.5 shows that mine has been in remission for some time, I'm going to take an ounce of it every few days as a preventive. Like I mention under garlic, I take two garlic pills every day as a preventive, and I haven't had a cold in about six years. If garlic can do that, I don't see why Essiac can't do the same thing.

Maybe the cancer of mine is all gone. I certainly take enough precautions with my eating and with all of the supplements I take. But just in case one should slip into me somehow, I want to have that Essiac there, ready and waiting for him.

I believe that people ill with any type of sickness, and including AIDS above all, who, using a change of diet and adding supplements to their daily fare and also start taking the Essiac tea, would see a marked improvement in their life.

I am not prescribing anything but just stating what I would do if I were in their place.

My First Steps to Health

As I mentioned earlier, I wrote a letter about Dr. R. to the local paper, and they published it. My mailman, who is one of the sweetest, kindest black men you would ever want to meet, knocked on my door one day. He said he had read my letter and told me to hang in there. This was way before I found out about PSA blood tests and Essiac. He gave me some material on apple cider vinegar that he had mimeographed. He said it was very good for you. I thanked him and put it on top of my dresser and forgot about it.

A few weeks later, I was at the airport, parked in line waiting for a fare. As usual, I had my supply of scandal sheets with me. I don't know if it was in *The Enquirer* or *The Examiner* or which one it was, but in one of them I ran across an article about apple cider vinegar. The doctors gave one tablespoon of apple cider vinegar and one tablespoon of honey to "X" amount of people and some kind of placebo to a similar amount of people three times a day. It stated that in a very short time, the people receiving the vinegar and honey had their arthritis go away. They cut out the placebo and gave everyone the vinegar and honey. Diabetics should just use the vinegar.

I went home and dug out the literature that Ivery had given me. After reading it, I decided to get some of that vinegar and try it out. A word of warning at this point. Never, ever use the white vinegar, and never buy it at the grocery store where it has been processed and all of the residue from the apples is taken out. That is the part that does all of the good. You have to get raw, unfiltered apple cider vinegar at the health food stores. There are several brands on the market. I use Spectrum's Natural because it is the mildest and easiest to take.

I used to take one tablespoon in a glass of water three times a day but now I just take two or more tablespoons once a day.

After several weeks of taking it, the pain from the arthritis in both of my knees and one finger went away. What a relief. I could now take long walks and peddle around on a bicycle. It was as if a miracle had happened.

Apple cider vinegar goes to all of the joints and dissolves the crystals and junk that have accumulated there. It then takes it to the blood stream where it dissolves. It is washed into the kidneys, along with all of the other waste and cholesterol that it found in the bloodstream.

Because of this cleansing action, the cholesterol goes down and the blood becomes thinner, causing it to flow more easily, and thus it takes a lot of the pressure off of the heart. It has no side effects as do the thinning drugs prescribed by doctors.

I have four sisters who are older than me. I am sixty-nine years old. My next sister is Ann ▆▆▆▆▆, and she is seventy-one. Rose ▆▆▆▆▆ is next in line at seventy-three. Katherine ▆▆▆▆ is next at seventy-five, and Martha is the oldest eighty. As you can tell by the ages, they are in the age group that has a lot of aches and pains. They have arthritis, diabetes, and Rose supposedly has Parkinson's, which I cover in another chapter. They also include heart trouble, high blood pressure, and just about every other ailment that you can think of between the four of them.

I burned up the telephone lines talking to all of my sisters, telling them all about the miracle of apple cider vinegar.

I told some of my cab driver buddies about the vinegar. One of them by the nickname Mush later told me that it cured the arthritis in his shoulder. He said that he had been having trouble lifting his arm above his shoulder, but since taking the vinegar, he has regained all of the motion and freedom of movement as he had had before.

I was in to take another physical, and I told the doctor that examined me about the vinegar. He was very interested, as he said his fingers were starting to stiffen up on him. I gave him the name and then told him to take it twice a day with honey. Some time later I ran into him. I asked him how his fingers were. He flexed them, like a pianist loosening up before a recital, and told me that all of the stiffness had gone away. I was sure getting a kick out of helping people to feel better.

1992
Garlic

I was in the health food store one day when I spotted a book about garlic. I bought a copy and took it home to read[2].

I had heard somewhere that garlic helped in curing a cold, but I sure was surprised with all of the other things it helped with. Some years ago there was an article in the Russian paper telling people to eat more garlic because of a deadly flu going around.

Some of the things that it did were:
Lower blood cholesterol
Prevent coronary artery disease
Prevent colds and flu
Fight cancer
Fight AIDS
Lower blood pressure
Enhance the immune system
Protect and help cure the liver
Earache
Eczema

Blind luck guided me when I went back to the health food store to purchase some garlic. I picked out Kyolic, and most health food books that mention garlic use Kyolic as the garlic of choice.

I immediately told my sisters Ann and Kay about it. They are the two that have diabetes. Ann started using it immediately whenever she cheated on her diet. She was amazed at how fast it brought her blood sugar down. She usually used four of the capsules at a time, and that did the trick.

As I mentioned earlier, I live in Anchorage and she lives in McKeesport, Pennsylvania. One day I got a telephone call from her, and she was very upset. She thought she had taken eight garlic capsules that day and was afraid that they would hurt her. I assured her that she had nothing to worry about, just so it wasn't that amount of raw garlic. That much is very, very bad for the system.

A lot of people that I have talked to about garlic mention that they use a lot of garlic when they cook. I point out to them that using garlic that way is good for the taste of the food, but then it loses its medicinal value.

In the first ten years or so that I drove cabs around Anchorage, I used to be hit with a lot of colds and flu. I would have to get out of my warm cab and go out in the cold to knock on doors looking for my passengers.

A lot of times I would pick up some Eskimo at the airport who just came in from Kotzebue, Barrow, or Fairbanks, where the temperature was fifty below. The first thing they would do would be to roll down the window and complain about the heat.

Sometimes it would take me five minutes or so, with the zero degree wind blowing on my back, before I could convince them to close the window. Sometimes I got the flu and a cold so bad that I had to lay on my back in bed with cotton in my nostrils to try to stop my nose from running. It was nothing for me to miss a week or so of work when that happened, and it happened quite frequently.

Alter reading that book and finding out how garlic helped to build up the immune system and fought the flu and colds, I decided to start taking two capsules every day as a preventive. I haven't had a cold or the flu since then and that has been about six years ago.

Whenever I get a little tickle in my throat, which is

the sign that a cold is trying to take hold, I immediately head for my garlic pills. I take four of them at a time, three times a day.

I then head for my apple cider vinegar. I put one tablespoon in a glass of warm water, gargle, and then spit it out. I do this every half hour or so all evening. This is usually enough to stop the cold dead in its tracks.

Whenever I get gays in my cab I tell them how garlic built up my immune system, and that if I practiced their lifestyle I would take garlic, Kyogreen and Essiac Tea to build up my immune system as a preventive.

1992
Barley - Kyogreen

I heard a knock on my door one day and when I opened it, there stood Ivery, my mailman. He said that he had some reading material for me. He told me that I would find a lot of useful information in the material. He also added that barley was very good in fighting cancer.

The books[3] all said that the juice of green barley leaves contains enzymes, proteins, potassium, and chlorophyll, which have an amazing restorative effect on the body. Barley juice also contains vitamins and minerals.

There are several varieties of barley drinks on the market. I chose Kyogreen because, along with the barley, it has wheat germ, kelp, and rice, plus Kyolic is made by the same people.

I noticed that I had a tremendous amount of energy as soon as I started drinking it.

Some of the things that Kyogreen help are:

         Allergies - congestion, hay fever, and hives
         Respiratory problems - pneumonia
         Asthma
         Cancer - breast, colon, abdominal, and chemotherapy relief
         Blood pressure
         Detoxification and cleansing
         Bowels regulated
         Reinforce the immune system

Sometimes I put a heaping teaspoon in a glass of distilled water and just drink it. It has a very nice taste and goes down quite easily. It looks just like instant coffee, only it is green. Other times I would put it into apple juice.

When I first started taking the Kyogreen, I took three big, heaping tablespoons a day. This immediately started a detoxifying effect in my body.

People don't realize how much junk and toxins there are that stay in our colons and body cells and don't want to come out. They say that when you get a colonic, which is an enema administered by a professional, that parasites, worms, and tapeworms, that have been inside of people for years, come out. I know that if I were a fat, old worm, nestled in some warm, damp spot with a constant supply of food, I would think that I was in heaven and never want to leave.

Before Kyogreen, I used to drink two cups of coffee in the morning to get my colon primed, and then I would head for the bathroom with a magazine or a crossword puzzle and a pack of cigarettes. I would sit there sometimes for a half hour or so, waiting and praying for the coffee to do its work.

Once the Kyo kicked in, my body started to let loose all of the junk that it had accumulated over the many years. The smell and stink in that bathroom was so bad and there was so much gas, that I was afraid to light a cigarette in case of an explosion.

It took about three days before the smell started to get better. It took about that long for my body to get rid of all that junk and toxins. I was going to the bathroom quite frequently at first. In fact, I didn't dare stray too far away from one. I cut down on the dosage I was taking and that made it a little easier on me, but I didn't quit. The light-headedness I was experiencing during the detoxification went away. With the changes I have made in my diet, plus the Kyo, I don't have any trouble with constipation any more.

About five hours after I go to bed, I usually come

awake from noise around the apartment. That is when I take my first drink of Kyo. I go back to bed and when I wake up for good, my body is charged up and I am ready to go.

I also found out that I didn't need the coffee anymore. I now drink one or two cups of hot water with honey in it, which gives me added energy.

My neighbor's brother came down from Kotzebue to have an operation for colon cancer. His mother stopped by my apartment and mentioned it. She said he would sit in the bathroom for hours trying to go, but he couldn't because of the cancer. I gave her some of my apple cider vinegar, garlic pills, and Kyogreen to give to him. She came over the next day and told me he was so relieved to have a bowel movement without pain.

He continued to take those things for the next ten days or so before his operation, and he just sailed through it. His mother said he went through it quite easily and that he didn't lose any of his hair from the chemotherapy.

I told quite a few people about the vinegar, garlic and Kyo as I drove them around in my cab, and a lot of them started on it. I got a very good feeling when someone came back and told me how much it helped them. One quite heavy-set black girl, who worked and had a very active boy, told me that it made quite a difference in her life. She said that it used to take her an hour to get herself moving in the morning. After she started to take the Kyo, she said that she just keeps puttering away all day long. She also said that instead of taking it all at once, she takes a little bit of it at a time, all during the day.

Another divorced, working mother with a twelve-year-old daughter was also very happy with the Kyo. She said that the girls in the office were amazed at the change in her attitude. She said that they asked her why she was walking around the office all peppy, cheerful, and happy, compared to the way she used to be. She told them that they would change too, if all of a sudden they had a lot more energy and the pain in their hip went away. She told me that she had hip pain for years, but now it was all gone.

I sent garlic pills and Kyo back home to all four of my sisters and got them started on it. I know definitely that Martha is still taking it, after the four years or so that it has been since then. One good thing about having ailing sisters like I do is that I get immediate results on everything I send them. I also find out if they work.

I was at the health food store shortly after this, standing in back of a fellow about my age. The cashier was in the back of the store helping another customer look for something, and so we had to wait. I looked down on the counter and he had a bottle of apple cider vinegar and a bottle of Kyogreen sitting there ready to purchase.

I said to him, "I see you use the same things that I do." He then told me that in the last 10 years he had three operations for cancer and that all that kept him going was the apple cider vinegar and Kyogreen. I mentioned my prostate operation, and then he asked me if I took anything else. I told him about the garlic pills. He told me he would give them a try and went back to pick some up.

Ivery, the mailman, sure did me a very big favor, because both of the things he got me started into turned out to be super cancer fighters.

1992
Canned Food

My sometimes roommate is a dancer by the name of JoAnn. When I met her she was working at the Bush Company, which is world famous and is one of the main tourist attractions here in Anchorage. Beautiful girls from all over the world come there to dance in the summertime because of the money to be made from the tourists. In the summer the town is packed with tourists from around the world who come to hunt, fish, and just sightsee. Most of them have already heard about the Bush Company from other tourists, and so have it on their agenda of things to do in Anchorage.

I met JoAnn through driving her back and forth to work in my cab and we became platonic friends. Every time she had a fight with her boyfriend she would come over to my house, sleep on my couch for a day or two and then leave when her anger subsided.

At the time I met her my eating habits were atrocious. About two hundred yards from my apartment was a restaurant, and right down the street was a hamburger joint. At the restaurant I would usually order an omelet with bacon and sausage on the side. Sometimes I would have hash brown potatoes or substitute pancakes instead. There was always a big glob of margarine on the plate which, after spreading on the pancakes, I would soak in maple syrup.

The next day I would stop by the hamburger joint and pick up an order to take back to my apartment. It consisted of two double meat cheeseburgers, either with French fries or onion rings, and a large Pepsi. Other times I would open a can of Beanie Weanies, which were little hot dogs, open a can of pork and beans and eat those while chewing on a bologna sandwich.

One day JoAnn said to me, "I'm tired of watching you eat all that garbage." She then made me take her to the grocery store where we bought stew meat and a bunch of vegetables. She then showed me how to make vegetable stew. When I was done with my first bowl I asked for more it was so good. From then on I was hooked and started to make stew myself.

One day while I was shopping at the grocery store I spotted some chicken broth. I thought I would use it instead of the beef in my next stew. This way I would have a variety and I wouldn't have to cut up the meat. I'm lazy.

I put all the vegetables into a big pot and then added two cans of chicken broth. It was so good that I ate the whole big pot in one day. I continued to do so quite frequently as it was so good. I thought that I was eating healthy food for a change.

One day I was into the VA for some reason or another. While you are waiting they always take your temperature and blood pressure. The nurse told me that my blood pressure was quite high. I think she said it was 152 over 95. I was shocked because I had never had any trouble with my blood pressure before, and since I started eating all those vegetables I figured that I should be in fine shape.

When I got home I got out the two cans of chicken broth I had in the cabinet. When I looked on the label under Sodium it read 1200 mg. I didn't need to check any further. I had found where my high blood pressure came from. I went to the food market and looked on the backs of a lot of different products that they had in cans. Every one of them had a very high sodium content. I have never bought any canned food since, except for *Del Monte* tomato sauce with no salt added. It has a sodium content of only 20 mg. I use it in my vegetable stew. I also use it when I cook up a pot of beans, into which I also add two carrots, two pieces of celery, a couple of small onions, about three cloves of garlic, and some *Dash* non-salt seasoning.

I make a very large pot of beans. Enough so that I can fill up five plastic, microwave-safe containers. I put them in the freezer of my fridge, and take them out as needed. Less cooking that way.

I started swallowing garlic pills like crazy. It didn't take very long and my blood pressure was back down to normal.

JoAnn always claims that she was the one that got me started on my health kick. I always agree with her, but I have never told her about that chicken broth.

1993
Oils

I made a mad dash for my fridge after reading what butter and margarine did to your body, and especially your heart. I had a package of each one, and I threw them both into the garbage can.

At the supermarket, I now check the labels listing the contents of each product. If one of the listings mentions partially hydrogenated oil, I drop it like a hot potato and start looking at other products to put into my grocery cart.

The book[4] said that the body needs fat, which it calls essential fatty acids, and the body's lack of these lead to cancer, diabetes, arthritis, and a list of other ills.

It stated that the use of saturated fats, rancid fats, processed oils, and altered fats lead to cancer.

After reading these statements is when I made my dash to the fridge to get rid of my butter and oleo as fast as possible.

The book then went on to say that there were various fats that the body needed for its use in its job of keeping you healthy. It said that they are all kept in dark bottles so that light couldn't get in and ruin the oil. They should be kept in the refrigerator at all times, and they can also be frozen for up to one year.

It also stated that flaxseed oil, the only one used in the treatment of cancer, has been very successful in doing so.

In reading through the various articles and seeing a lot of technical terms that I did not understand, I resorted to my favorite tactic.

Whenever I go to the health food store to buy

anything, here's what I do. After finding the location of the object, be they vitamin, mineral, or whatnot, I call the health clerk over. Then I ask her which one of these brands is your best seller; that's the one I buy.

We have very knowledgeable people in our health food stores, and after locating them in the large built-in refrigerator where she had them, I questioned her.

She said that after flaxseed oil, which is the best, there are these: Hemp oil, borage, canola, sesame, safflower, and olive oil.

I mentioned that I was already taking the flaxseed, but I was thinking of adding another one as well.

She said that was a good idea, and that's what she did. She then recommended hemp oil, which I bought in spite of its slightly higher cost. I'm glad I did because when I got home and drank a tablespoon of it, I went OOOOOmmmm. It has a sweet, nutty taste and is delicious.

She told me that a person gets all the oil they need in three tablespoons a day, and not to exceed that amount. I told her that I would take two spoons of the flax and one tablespoon of the hemp one day, and then vice versa the next day.

She said not to use any of these oils for cooking, for once cooked, they are then hazardous to your health.

She then took a container out of the fridge and told me that this is what she used for her cooking. It was grape seed oil.

She then showed me some Ghee clarified butter, which was not only good for cooking, but was very good when spread on bread. I bought the grape seed oil for my cooking, for when I ever broke down and did some. I also bought the Ghee to spread on my bread so that I could alternate it with the olive oil I was now using.

Not only did I save myself a lot of time and effort, but the facts that she told me were more accurate than if I would have tried to sort them out from the book.

1993
Health Food - Junk Mail

When I ordered some vitamins through the mail, I must have found my way onto every health food publication in this country. But unlike most people who hate junk mail, I welcomed it with open arms.

I received many offers of health products that were supposed to enrich my life.

I received offers from many doctors who, having started out as traditional doctors and had gotten disenchanted with it, turned to alternative medicine. They made appeals for me to buy their monthly newsletters.

These newsletters contained just enough useful information to keep you reading, with promises of more useful news if you bought their publication. If I saw a product mentioned in two or more of these letters, I would go to the health food store and buy a book on that product. This way, I learned more and more about health food products, vitamins, and supplements.

I finally decided to subscribe to one of the newsletters. It seemed like one of the best ones I had received. The name is *Health and Healing* by Dr. Julian Whitaker, published by Phillips Publishing, Inc., 7811 Montrose Road, Potomac, MD 20854. I couldn't have made a better choice, as I have received much helpful advice from this monthly newsletter.

I have made additional purchases through the advertisements I received. One of them was a product called "Yohimbe." It is advertised as a sexual enhancement for the older male. I bet I have received at least ten letters from different companies trying to sell me sexual enhancement products. I found out that I could buy it cheaper at the local health food store.

I now use "Men's High Potency Zinc Formula," which I found at a GNC store. Not only does it do the trick, but the zinc is also very good for your eyes.

So if you want to learn about health food products, order something from one of the companies, then just wait for the health mail to come pouring in.

1993
Water

I used to read a lot of science fiction but, after being bitten by the health bug, my field of interest changed. I started buying health books. After I read in them what had been done to our food and water supply, I made quite a few rapid changes. The books all told how chlorine was very bad for the body.

When it came to fluoride, I was really shocked. One book[5] told of how fluoride was made of aluminum dust and the body couldn't assimilate it. Even I was smart enough to figure that out.

Then they went on to say that when the people who had died of Alzheimers disease had their heads cut open at autopsies they found a lot of aluminum. Since the moment I read that sentence, I have never drank any tap water. I started buying distilled water at the local store. At $1.25 a gallon, this proved quite expensive. My buddy Fred told me about a store that sold water purifiers, and also filled up your empty containers for 50¢ each. I started taking ten empty containers there at a time to get refilled.

After a while, I got tired of making so many trips and, since I had a few extra dollars at the time, I decided to invest in a water purifier. I bought one that is only about two feet by two feet and sits on the counter by the sink. You attach a hose to your faucet, the water runs through the purifier, and in three or four hours you have about a two gallon supply.

Several years ago there were front page stories about Hoonah, Alaska. I guess that when they add the fluoride to the water supply they have to regulate it so that only a certain amount of fluoride gets into X amount of gallons of water. It seems that the motor that did this job broke down so that too much fluoride got into the water. A lot of people got sick and two died. Does that tell you something? The FDA lets it in because they say it is good for children's teeth. If people, especially children, would cut down on meat, sugar, and soda pop, and get enough calcium in their diets, they wouldn't have any tooth problems. And all of us older people wouldn't get that junk into our systems.

Some time ago, there was an article in the paper about chlorine. One of the representatives in Washington stood up while the Congress was in session and read a report about all of the bad things that chlorine was doing to people's bodies. It seems that, not only did the chlorine kill a lot of bacteria in the water supply, it was killing a lot of people, too. It was proven to cause a variety of diseases in man, one of which was rectal cancer. His report went on to state that the scientific community had nothing to replace chlorine in the purification of water.

I have read no more about this report. Maybe they are working to find a replacement for chlorine, or maybe, since chlorine is used in so many products on the market and there is so much money involved for the manufacturers of chlorine, their lobbyists may have squelched any action on this matter.

One final report I read in the paper was about the cost of distilled water in the government offices in Washington. I don't remember if the figure was $200,000 or two million for all of that distilled water. If you take into account how many of them there are and how thirsty they must get after some of those long wind bag speeches that they give, you have to believe the figure was two million.

Doesn't the fact that the congressmen are now

drinking all of this distilled water give you the urge to do likewise?

1993
Meat & Veggies

Just about every health book that I read spelled out the evils of meat and what it did to your body. They claimed it was the cause of most of man's illnesses, from obesity to diabetes, heart disease, arthritis, cancer, and just about every one that was left after that.

They also said that meat, along with white bread, didn't have any fiber to them. They would get to the colon and just stay there, thus causing constipation. Matter left in the colon too long causes colon cancer.

When I was young, there wasn't so much cancer as there is now. Of course, in those days, they didn't put any antibiotic or growth hormones into the cattle, as they do now.

In the 1940s, they came out with a whole lot of antibiotics. When a cow or steer got sick, they would give it some of these new antibiotics. They soon found out that not only did they heal the cow, they also made it grow a whole lot faster. From then on, all cows were automatically given shots of antibiotics and growth hormones at birth. The faster the cow grew, the more money the rancher made. Good old Yankee ingenuity.

Of course, when we drank the cow's milk, we got the drugs into our bodies. When they butchered those cows, we got the rest of those drugs. Along with those drugs and the fat in the meat, our troubles grew.

I know this has been written about by a lot of people with more brains than I have, and most people already know these facts. It's just that when I read about them, they were all new to me.

One time I glanced through a book written by

vegetarians who didn't eat any meat, fish or chicken. On the spur of the moment, I decided that I was going to do the same thing. I gave up all three of those, just like they did, even though I loved fish and ate chicken occasionally.

That was the worst mistake I had made in a long time, and believe me, I had made many of them in my lifetime.

To become a true vegetarian, you have to read countless books on how to cook and combine certain things like beans and rice and such, to get all of the protein that your body needs.

In a short time, I became listless and weak. I decided to call one of Martha's daughters, Cindy. She lives in San Francisco, and I heard she was into healthy living and eating.

After I explained my situation to her, she told me the answer to my problem. She said that since you are too lazy to cook, you have to eat a little fish to get some protein into you. She said that as little as a can of sardines, which is 3 ounces, eaten every other day, was enough.

She also advised me to get some sublingual B12 pills. I was lacking in this because of the lack of animal flesh.

Since it was late, the health food store was closed, and I had to buy the B12 at a drug store. The druggist told me that the body only used as much as it needed and got rid of the rest through the kidneys. I bought the smallest bottle that the drug store had, as I only intended using it until I got to a health food store and could buy the good stuff. I never buy any of my vitamins or supplements at the drug stores. Let those pharmaceutical companies keep all of their junk. I read somewhere that the body didn't absorb a lot of their stuff and just passed it on through the colon.

I also read in one of Dr. Whitaker's articles that as we get older, we need more B12 for extra energy. I now take KAL 2000 for my B12 needs. It has a very nice taste and is easy to take.

I took the B12 and ate a can of sardines that evening. In the morning, I was my old self again. I am now back to eating the salmon and halibut that I love.

I also, on occasion, ate a little chicken. The books said that you should eat the breast only, as it was the leanest. I prefer the thighs, and that is what I ate.

One day while getting my hair trimmed (I didn't have too much to cut), I got into a conversation with the barber. He told me that once he went to visit his brother-in-law who raised chickens for a living. He raised forty thousand of them at a time and was making a lucrative living from them.

His brother-in-law took him for a tour of his chicken ranch. As they walked, he heard one chicken give a loud squawk and jump about four feet up into the air. When the chicken hit the ground, it was dead.

When he asked his brother-in-law what happened, he replied, "In order to get the chickens to grow faster, we give them growth hormones." The barber then said, "Isn't that bad?" his brother-in-law replied. "No, it's good. With the growth hormones, they grow twice as fast as they used to, and so I make more money." He added that once in a while, the growth hormone caused the chicken to have a heart attack as he just witnessed, but it was no big deal. Where was the Society for the Prevention of Cruelty to Animals?

No more chicken for me, unless purchased at the health food store.

I started to slowly change my eating habits. I threw out candy bars, donuts, pies, white bread, and anything made of white flour. This included supermarket pasta. When I read they were made with enriched flour, I realized then that they did with it as they did with so many other products on the grocery shelves. In order to get a longer shelf life, they grind and mill it, or whatever other processes they have, to take the vitamins and such out of it that would spoil fast. Then they put synthetic vitamins into it and called it new and enriched. The health food stores carry pasta that is ten times better for you.

I'll bet that if there were an atomic war and if all of the people were wiped out, leaving earth a desolate planet, this is what would happen. In a thousand years, a spaceship full of aliens from outer space would land, and this is what they would find on the shelves of supermarkets still standing. All the food on the shelves that had preservatives in them would taste like they had just been put on the shelves that morning and would just melt in your mouth.

I started eating rice, pasta, grains (by grains I mean bread that has multi grains in them and no preservatives — I'm too lazy to do any real cooking), nuts, seeds, fruit and vegetables.

I had read somewhere that olive oil tasted good on potatoes and bread. I skeptically decided to try some and was amazed at how good it tasted. Besides which, olive oil is good for you.

I have always loved yams and sweet potatoes, and now even more so when I read what Dr. Whitaker had to say about them. His report states that yams and sweet potatoes contain DHEA, which fights aging. DHEA is produced by the adrenal gland, and as we age it makes less and less of it. He says that by increasing our levels of DHEA, we can decrease most of the known makers of aging. I now eat yams and sweet potatoes as often as possible.

Since I don't especially like to cook, I try to make it as easy on myself as I can, when I do so.

I bought a combination rice and vegetable steamer at Wal-Mart that was fairly reasonably priced. The book that comes with it shows the cooking instructions for a wide variety of foods you can cook with it and how long to set the timer for.

For rice, you just put your rice and water in an insert they provide. Put it into the steamer and set the timer for fifty-five minutes. In fifty-five minutes, a little bell goes ping, and you know they're done. No fuss, no muss.

The steamer part for vegetables is really a work saver. At the grocery store, they have frozen veggies that come three or four different kinds to a package. I buy three bags containing different varieties of veggies. When I go to cook them, I put a little from each bag in at the same time. Not only do I get my share of vitamins from these veggies that are good for me, but they are delicious. Sometimes I add a little bit of "Dash," a saltless seasoning.

Two of the best fish in Alaska are halibut and salmon. If you asked ten Alaskans walking down the street what was the best way to cook halibut, you would get ten different answers, as everyone has their own secret recipe. Once again, I cook mine the easy way. I put it in the microwave for three minutes on each side. If it is not completely white and flaky, I put it in for another minute or so. Sometimes I add a little "Dash" to it. Fast, easy, and it is delicious. Do not overcook, as overcooking dries it out and takes away most of the taste and flavor.

For salmon, I put a piece of it on a dish and put it in the oven. I do not preheat the oven, but just put it on bake and set the temperature at 350 degrees F. After twenty or twenty-five minutes, depending on the thickness of the salmon you are cooking, check out the fish. If there are white globules of fat on top of it, it is done. Do not over cook. Alaska salmon doesn't need seasoning of any kind. When you put the first bite into your mouth, it literally melts.

A lot of people are eating farm-raised salmon. They put a lot of herbs and spices on it and rave about how good it tastes. What tastes good to them are those herbs and spices.

I bought some in a supermarket in Pittsburgh on one of those visits. It tasted like cardboard when I cooked it my way, and I spit it out and threw it away.

1994
Juice Fasting

I picked up a book on juice fasting from the health store. In it were glowing reports of the benefits of juicing. It said that the body has a certain amount of energy, and most of that is used in the digestion of food. When you take nothing but juice into your body, it uses all of this extra energy that it all of a sudden has to clean out and repair itself.

It said that you were to eat lightly for a few days before your juice diet began. It warned that you could expect some nausea on the third or fourth day but that it would pass, and not to exceed ten days of fasting the first time that you started into fasting. It said that you break the fast gradually. The first day you eat a small salad and one small apple, while still continuing with the juices. The second day, you eat a large salad and two apples, plus juices. The third day you resume eating, being careful not to overeat and gain all of your weight right back. It also said that you had to take an enema twice a day, once in the morning and once before going to bed. This was to make sure that all of the toxins that your body was expelling wouldn't get reabsorbed into the blood stream.

I went out and bought a small juicer at Sears, and then I went to the grocery store and stocked up on vegetables, apples, and grapes. The body uses the vegetable juice to clean and repair itself and the fruit juices to carry the debris into the blood stream and then out of the body.

Apple juice and grape juice are wonderful for the cleansing. Not only do they clean, but they both have a lot of potassium, which the body needs. When you juice them, you must make sure that you dilute them half and half with pure distilled water. I didn't do it once with the grape juice, and it went right through me.

All you need is one glass of either of these juices a day.

I didn't know too much about what veggies to use, so I mixed a bunch of the different veggies together and drank it. I put in carrots, celery, potatoes, cabbage, green peppers, beets, and everything else that was available. One time I even put in some rhubarb. Boy, that really spoiled that batch. I had no set amount of the juice to drink. After all, it stands to reason that the more vitamins and minerals that the body had to work with, the faster it would work.

The first time I juiced, the only things that I took with it were the apple cider vinegar, garlic pills, and Kyogreen, twice a day. Every time I got an urge to eat, I would put a little bit of honey on a spoon, and after I ate it, that seemed to stop my craving for food.

In order to keep from having to juice all day long, I started making enough to fill a big pitcher full. I didn't find out for a long time, but that was a big no-no. First, juice should be drunk as soon as possible after making them, or they start to lose their vitamins. The second and most important reason was, cabbage and certain other veggies start to oxidize shortly after they are juiced and are then very harmful to your body.

The first two days went by easily enough. On the third and fourth days, the reaction from what those juices were doing to me commenced. I was nauseous, light-headed, weak, and I walked around in sort of a fog. The only thing that kept me from quitting the juice fast was the amount of weight I was losing. My body started expelling its debris not only through my colon, but through my pores and tongue. I had to shower quite frequently, as I got to feeling dirty. My tongue developed a thick, white coat. I used a spoon to scrape it off.

From the fifth day on, the fog started to lift and the other symptoms became easier to live with.

On the ninth day, I had such a surge of energy go through my body that it was unbelievable. I was so charged up that I wanted to jump up and down and to run everywhere instead of walking.

The tenth day was more of the same, only more so. My body felt like I was eighteen years old again and that I could leap mountains. I quit juicing because the book said only 10 days.

I lost twenty pounds, but something else happened that proved all of those claims that the body repaired itself while you were fasting.

In 1965, I married this girl who had three children. They were aged 9, 14, and 15. I purchased a used house trailer from a friend of mine and went about the business of raising a family.

Shortly after we purchased it, we started having trouble with the water heater. I didn't know how to relight it when it went out, so this job fell to my wife. One day she said to me, "I'm getting tired of lighting this darn heater back up. You're the man of the house, and I'm going to teach you how to do it." She then proceeded to show me how to do it.

The first time that I lit it, it worked perfectly. The second time was a different story. As I put the match into the opening, I heard a loud pop. Some instinct must have told me to close my eyes, which I did. A big ball of flame shot out and hit me right in the face. It singed my hair in the front and along the sides. It burned me across the nose and under both eyes. There were also little burn marks on both sides of my face.

Since it was late at night, we called our doctor at his home. He told me to just keep a cold cloth on it and it would be all right in the morning. In a few days, all the pain went away, and I just treated the burns as if they weren't there.

When my friends saw me after my juice diet, I got quite a few remarks on how my complexion had cleared up. The burns under my eyes had gotten a whole lot lighter, and the little burn marks on both sides of my face had gone away. I have juiced a total of four times now, and it seems the burns under my eyes get lighter ever time.

My fourth time that I juiced was a snap. I had learned of the right supplements to take while doing so. The more you take of supplements that your body needs, and give you energy, the easier it is to get through the fast. Anyone can do this fast if they take the following:

A good multi vitamin pill - I use Dr. Whitaker's Forward

CO Q 10, good for heart and lots of energy

Liquid potassium with magnesium, tablespoon twice a day

B12 can only get from meat, fish or chicken. Body must have it and sublingual is best

L-Carnitine, good for heart and has lots of energy

Apple cider vinegar to help purify the blood

Two Kyolic garlic pills

Two tablespoons of flaxseed oil

Teaspoon of Kyogreen twice a day

One chromium picolinate pill daily even when not on fast

Two cayenne pepper pills a day, heart and energy

Might be good idea to get doctor's okay first

If when you start juicing for the first time the shock to your body is too much for you, quit and try it in another week or two. This gives your body a chance to rest

up so that you can try again. The repairs that juicing does
to your body, combined with the weight loss, is well worth
a second try.

I also found a wonderful juice book entitled *Fresh
Vegetable and Fruit Juices* by N.W. Walker[6]. It is very well
written, and in it he tells you all about just about every
vegetable and fruit there is. In the back he tells you what
combinations of juices to use for each different ailment that
you are trying to correct. By following the amount of each
juice he prescribes for each drink, the drink turns out quite
tasty.

He even has a series of juices that he claims will
cure arthritis.

I bought a Champion juicer. You get more of the
vitamins and minerals out of your vegetable, and I could
tell right away by the taste and just by looking at it in the
glass. I found that I now needed only half as many carrots
as I did before, as all of the juice was now being extracted
and there was less waste. The savings on the vegetables
paid for the cost of the new juicer in a very short time.

When I used to smoke, I would always keep my
window open a few inches to let the smoke out. After years
of driving like that, the cold air blowing on my neck caused
arthritis to form there. Apple cider did not cure that. But
now, the pain is all gone. I didn't know whether to credit
this fact to the juicing or the Kyogreen.

1994
Earaches & Hearing - Tree Tea Oil

About three years ago, I had a woman passenger in my cab one day, and instead of me having a captive audience, the tables were reversed.

I can usually tell when I have a captive audience and they are interested in what I have to say.

If they are interested and start asking questions, or even give me some hint that they might be interested, there's no stopping me then.

If they sit there and say things like, "oh, yeah" or "uh-huh", I know that I would be wasting my time trying to talk to them. When that happens, I just let my eyes look around at our beautiful mountains or greenery until I drop my passenger off and go pick up a more appreciative audience.

As soon as I brought up the subject of health, she jumped right in and took over the talking, which usually was my job, but this time I didn't care.

She said that in raising her three children, she had her hand full on many occasions with the earaches that they were always getting.

She continued by saying that she was always in the doctor's office getting antibiotics for them. But she soon found out that the antibiotics were messing up the bacteria in their intestines.

She went to the health food store and asked them if they had anything for ear infections. The clerk led her to a shelf in the back where she took down a bottle which was labeled "ear drops."

She said she had also learned that a lot of earaches are caused by too much protein, mainly milk. She said that from then on out, whenever her kids started coming down with an earache, she would make them stop drinking milk. Then she would go get the ear drop bottle. She said that she would then follow the directions on the side of the bottle, telling her how many drops to put into the ear and how often.

She added that by following those directions and making sure that those kids didn't drink any milk, the infection would clear up in no time.

I asked her what was in the bottle of ear drops and she replied one had olive oil, garlic oil, and some herb that she couldn't recall the name of.

The other one had garlic oil and two different herbs. She said that she had success with either one of the bottles.

When we arrived at her destination, I thanked her and told her that I was going to go to the health food store and look for some of those ear drops. My ears had been causing me a little annoyance lately.

After I showered, it seemed that I could never get into my ear far enough with the towel to dry them completely, and that when they finally got air dried, they would start to itch. I told her that I was going to try them.

She said that I might find out that the ear drops might start to regenerate my ear, as that was what happened to her. When she said that, I could hardly wait for my shift to be over so that I could go home, get into bed, and when the night was over, I could hurry down to the health food store.

If at this point you figured out that I wanted to try the drops out on myself first and then on my sisters, you can hold your hand up and holler "bingo." I found the drops at the health food store with no trouble at all and started using them. At first I put five drops into my ears, twice a day. Then I cut down to once a day after the itching quit.

Besides the relief of not having itchy ears anymore, I found that my hearing was now better. The drops soften the wax, allowing the voices to get through easier.

When I first started driving, I would always yak at my passengers. It was so nice to be around someone who talked.

When I had people who were talking to each other, I would just sit there and listen as I drove them to their destination.

I found that as time went by that I could just tune my passengers out and would just concentrate on my driving. But a lot of times when they were passing some juicy tidbits back and forth between each other, they talked so low that I couldn't hear them, no matter how much I tried.

Now when they started whispering, I could hear all of their conversation. I guess there's a little bit of a "voyeur" in everybody. I never said I was an angel.

On my next trip home, I took three bottles of the ear drops with me. While looking through the reading section at one of our local health food stores, I had randomly picked out a book[7] about tree tea oil from the rack. In it, it tells of how the natives in Australia, who, when they got injured in any way where the flesh was cut, would hurry to certain trees and rub the oil from the tree leaves onto their wounds. These wounds then healed very quickly.

It then goes on to explain about how they eventually got around to harvesting and processing the leaves from these trees into oil. It said that since it helped wounds heal rapidly, it would be very helpful to diabetics.

In diabetics, the one big fear is of cuts or scratches

on their bodies. Their cuts and scratches don't heal very rapidly, and there is always the fear that gangrene would set in.

When I read this statement, I made sure that I had three bottles on my next trip home.

Whenever I go back to Pennsylvania for a visit, I always stay at Martha's place first. After first resting and visiting for a few days, I then visit my other sisters.

At eighty years of age, Martha is the oldest of my four sisters. Despite all the adversity that she has faced in her life, she has fought through it and faces life as if to say, "well, God, I got through that last stuff you sent my way and I'm standing here waiting for whatever other mischief you have in store for me."

The first evening of my arrival, we spent a short time talking before I headed for the bedroom. The long trip and jet lag had set in, and I was tired. I hadn't heard about Melatonin then. Airlines personnel in my cab say that they all use it to fight jet lag and aging.

The next morning I gave Martha a bottle of both the ear oil and the tree tea oil. Along with the other things I have mentioned about her in this book, she had ear and foot problems and had need for them.

Her hearing was very bad, so she immediately opened the bottle and put in five drops of the ear oil into each ear.

Years ago, an arthritis doctor had talked her into letting him operate on her toes in order to straighten them out. It seems that her arthritis had struck down there, too. To make a long story short, his botched operation left her with toes pointing every which way but straight ahead. Because of their being over and around each other, their constant friction caused open sores and infections.

She took her shoes off and put some on her toes

right away.

The next time I saw her after visiting my other sisters, she said she could now hear better and that the infection on her toes was healing and looked better than it used to.

I next went to visit Ann. One of her sayings used to be, "I'm deaf in one ear and can't hear out of the other one." One of her ears did have a ruptured ear drum. She thought she was going deaf in the other ear because she would many times cup her hand around her ear and ask you to speak up or repeat what you had just said.

Like Martha, she immediately put five drops of the oil in both ears. The next time I saw her, she told me of how much better her hearing had become.

She didn't have any use for the tea tree oil at that time but was very happy to have it in her medicine cabinet in case of an emergency.

A few days later I went to stay with sister Kay and her husband Cy, short for Sylvester. He always said his name should be "Shoulda" because Kay was always saying to him, "you shoulda did this," or "you shoulda did that." Really love his sense of humor and the jokes that he every once in a while comes up with.

Kay did the same thing that Ann did with the ear drops after I explained what it had done for my ears.

Like Ann, she had no immediate use for the tree tea oil then but placed it in her medicine cabinet for future use.

I returned to Martha's. After being home a few days, I decided to go to the East End Food Co-op. It is a health food store. If you're ever in the area and you want to meet a warm, pleasant, helpful girl, stop in and see Vicky who works there.

I wanted to pick up two more bottles of the ear

drops for my nieces. After getting the bottles for me, Vicky said, "we also have the ear candles that go with them." I had no idea of what she was talking about, as she could tell by the dumb look on my face, so she led me over to a shelf where they were on display.

Ear candles looked similar to regular candles, and so I guess that's how they got their name. They are hollow and made of a heavy paper which is covered with a light coating of wax. On the end of the candle, where the wick usually stuck out, was a small hole.

She tried to explain how it worked, but for me to understand something, you have to actually show me how it worked or show me a picture.

She went into her office and in a short time came out with a factory diagram showing how it worked. I really appreciated the time and effort she put in for me.

The diagram showed an aluminum plate, the kind you can buy in the supermarket, four or six to a package.

The chart explained that you cut a hole in the aluminum pan just big enough so that the tapered end of the candle that the wick normally comes out of could pass through. You put it in only about two inches.

Then the person who has had the ear oil in their ear for several days, to loosen the ear wax that accumulates there, lays on the bed. If the left ear is going to be cleaned first, he or she would lay in their right side, and then vice versa for the other ear.

Then the person on the bed places their hand over their ear, with their index and middle finger spread apart, so that the tapered end of the candle would fit through them and into the ear. A towel is then placed around the parts of the person's face that is not covered by the aluminum plate. The aluminum plate plus the towel are for protection so some stray piece of the burnt candle doesn't get on you when the person standing lights the end of the candle.

This is just an extra protection, and I have seen nothing get out on anybody I have used it on. The diagram said to have a small plate of water on hand, just in case, and I follow that rule, although I have never had any call to use it.

Then as I said above, the person standing lights the candle. Because of the wax on the candle, it burns very slowly. As the candle burns, the person wiggles it around until they hear a crackling sound; they then keep it positioned in that spot.

As the candle burns, it takes all of the air from the candle and this causes a suction to develop. This suction causes the wax in the ear to be sucked out and into the end of the candle.

The person standing watches, and as any stray ash begins to form, snips it off with a pair of scissors and puts it in an empty dish or any receptacle you have available.

When the candle is burnt down to about two or three inches from the aluminum plate, you take it out.

Then you cut the remaining part of the candle open, and you are amazed by the amount of wax that you have extracted.

Then you turn over and do the other ear.

I could hardly wait to try it out on the girls. I hurriedly drove to Ann's. After I explained the procedure to her, she eagerly lay down on the bed. After we finished and I started talking to her, she told me how much better she could now hear.

When I arrived at Martha's, I explained the procedure to her.

She said, "What the heck, let's try it out." After we did the first candle, we cut the remaining piece open and there lay a long streamer of wax. After we did the other ear, Martha, just as Ann, was very pleased with how much better she could hear.

At Kay's I was greeted with skepticism, so I asked Cy to try it on me. After we were done and Cy saw how much wax had come out of my ears, he made this remark: "If everyone in the country knew about this procedure, half of the people wouldn't need hearing aids."

At this point, they received a phone call and had to leave. I left them four of the candles and a plate, because they wanted to try it themselves.

I returned to Martha's. The phone rang, and Martha, who was busy doing something, hollered for me to answer it. I picked up the phone and said hello, and when the person on the other end started talking, I almost jumped out of my shoes. It sounded like they were hollering, and it scared the bejesus out of me.

On the plane taking me back to Anchorage, I sat there with a big smile on my face and with this thought in my mind: "Thank you Lord, Allah, Odin and all you other guys."

Warning: Be sure to use only ear candles purchased at the health food store for $2.00 each. The coat of wax on them makes them burn slowly. If you try to make your own with paper or any other material, the fire could burn down real fast and burn your ear drum.

Do not use on ears that have been punctured.

1994
Amino Acids

I was parked at the airport one day reading my favorite scandal sheets again when I ran across an article about Tom Arnold, Roseanne's husband. It said that he went to a specialist in amino acids who had given him something to curb his appetite and give him energy. That, plus a changed diet, some exercise, and he had lost forty pounds in a very short while.

The things he gave him were Chromium Picolinate, which I was already using. He also gave him L-Carnitine and L-Phenylalanine.

I went to the health food store and purchased some and got started on them right away.

I have since then seen an article about some scientists working with L-Phenylalanine as an anti-depressant. They should have me in their study, because everything that I have taken works on me right away.

I don't know how long it took for the pills to kick in — just a few days, I think. When they did, they had me walking on cloud nine. I had so much energy that I was doing my exercises four times a day. I couldn't believe the feeling of euphoria that I had. So much better than Valiums, Xanax, or all the drugs that are on the market.

This also was about the time that I was into the fourth time of juice fasting. I will go into juicing in another chapter, but I will just say that it made it so much easier. I was just filled with a super abundance of energy.

Many years ago, I used to play a game called low ball. In it, the low cards won instead of the high cards. In other words, one, two, three, four, five would be the best hand. One, two, three, four, six would be the next best hand, and so on up the line. I used to be very good at it and used to win most of the time.

Last year I decided that I would like to try playing cards again. I found out where the poker games were taking place, but when I got there, they told me that they didn't play low ball anymore. They said that they played a game called Texas Hold 'Em. It is a game similar to seven card stud. Each player is given two cards and then three cards are turned up in the middle of the table. You bet on those three cards, and then the dealer turns another card up and you bet again. You bet after the fifth and final card is turned up. The player that makes the best hand out of the seven cards wins.

Since I wanted to gamble and it looked so easy, I decided to play. By taking it easy, playing very carefully, and a whole bunch of luck, I found myself $250 ahead. This took about five hours, and as much as I wanted to keep playing, I had to quit because I was too sleepy.

The following Sunday I decided to try my luck again. In order to give myself a lot of energy to play for a long time and not get sleepy, I took the amino acids.

Not only did I have super energy and didn't get sleepy at all, I was once again floating on cloud nine. I forgot all about playing carefully, got into almost every pot, and lost all of the money I had on me. I drove home and got all of the money I had in the whole world, and went back to play some more cards. When the smoke had cleared, I found myself driving home broke. I had lost thirteen hundred dollars. But I was so high that I didn't care. In fact, I was singing all the way home.

The next day when I woke up, an old saying that I used to say after a bout of drinking came to my mind. "Never again." I quit taking the pills. It was easy to quit, as aminos are not addictive.

By now you realize that I do a lot of reading. If it's not scandal sheets or newspapers, it's health pamphlets or books that they sell at the health food stores. One of the books that caught my eye was, *All You Wanted to Know About Amino Acids*[8]. It was very interesting reading, and it had many different uses for amino acids.

In the book I also came across a line that said, "L-Phenylalanine takes iodine from the thyroid and converts it into other aminos that the body needs." Right then I realized why I was getting a slight pain and swelling below my left ear. Being that I didn't use salt, I wasn't getting my share of iodine, and so a goiter was starting to grow on my neck.

I went to the health food store and asked the girl what the daily intake of iodine should be. She looked it up on a chart she had and told me that the recommended amount was two hundred and fifty milligrams, but that you could safely take up to a thousand a day.

I bought a bottle of Icelandic Kelp, which contained not only iodine but a small amount of minerals, vitamins, and aminos. I took four of those pills a day for about a week to ten days, and the swelling and pain went away.

In the article that I read in the scandal sheet, it didn't say anything about taking iodine. I wonder how many people across the country read that article and as a result of a lack of iodine, developed goiters. It sure was a good thing that I read that book.

I can see how people that take drugs of any kind can easily get hooked, be it cocaine, marijuana, heroin, or prescription drugs.

If someone could perfect that formula with the aminos and give people the glowing feeling that I had, I'm sure we could wipe out the drug trade in this country. You could get enough aminos to keep you happy for about sixty dollars a month. The dopeheads pay fifty dollars for a half gram of cocaine, and that doesn't last for even one night. Just think of the amount of money that would be taken out of the hands of dope dealers and put into the economy. Also, we could empty out our jails that are mostly filled with people with drug convictions. There would be no more babies born with coke addictions from cokehead mothers, plus a whole bunch of other benefits, not counting the people who die of overdoses and deteriorated health because of the drugs.

One of the services that our cab company does is picking up orders for people who, for some reason, cannot or don't want to go to the store. We deliver cigarettes, groceries, and prescriptions.

Whenever I am sent to a pharmacy, I jokingly say to the pharmacist, "How about a couple of Valiums, Xanaxes, or pain killers for a tip?" I tell him that I want to go to seventh heaven for a while. He smiles, but no luck. They are just as bad as cocaine because people who, when they start to take them, don't know the addictive power that they hold.

I just recently did an eight-day juice fast. In order to make the juicing easier on me, I took the amino acids again. Although they gave me a lot of energy, they didn't get me high like they did a year ago. Maybe the fact that I have added minerals and other supplements to my daily intake has made up for some deficiency in my body that caused the euphoria I got from the aminos.

My shift of driving cab is from five in the afternoon until two or three in the morning. The younger guys drive for twelve hours but nine or ten is enough for me.

In the wintertime when our long dark days role in I

get home when it is dark and then go back to work when it is just getting dark. Consequently I develop a form of depression known as Seasonal Affective Disorder (SAD).

I read an article that said that one third of Alaskans suffer this form of depression. Many of whom will turn to eating more, drinking more and a lot of them to suicide.

That is why so many Alaskans gain weight in the winter. You develop a craving for sweet starchy food.

I used to have an obsession with Raisin bagels. I used to cut them in half, toast them, and then put a generous amount of Olive oil on them. Just melt in your mouth.

I used to get these feelings towards the end of November. I would talk less to my customers, eat more and get thoughts of moving out of Alaska.

About four years ago when this feeling set in I started saving my money because I was going to leave as soon as the busy season was over.

My buddy Fred had a going away party for me. I gave up my apartment, sold anything that couldn't fit into two suitcases and moved out.

I stayed in the lower forty-eight for two months but I couldn't stand it and that was enough for me. I got on the plane and returned north.

When Fred saw me he said, "Christ what are you doing back? I thought we got rid of you."

The next year when I went through this same depression I didn't tell anyone I was moving out. I just said that I was going on vacation.

Paid a few months rent on my apartment, kept the phone and utilities working, but did call Prime Cable to put me on vacation mode.

Two months later when I returned I said thank the gods that I kept my apartment and didn't have to go through the hassle of getting started all over again.

Once I realized what was happening to me every winter and finding out about Amino acids I knew what to do.

I get out my L-Phenylalanine and take one 500 mg of them three times a day on an empty stomach. In no time at all my depression is lifted and I am my happy smiling self again.

If I could just get that feeling of euphoria that I got when I first started using them I'd really be happy.

1994
DLPA 750

About three months ago I was in the health food store browsing through their books. The clerk gave me a pamphlet on DLPA 750[9]. The pamphlet said that it was made up of a combination of D-Phenylalanine and L-Phenylalanine.

The L-Phenylalanine was 375 mg and it was a mood enhancer.

The D-Phenylalanine was 375 mg and it was a pain killer.

It stated that when you take the capsule, they separate with the one going to your brain to lift depression, and the other going through your body to suppress pain.

It stated that the D-Phenylalanine was so powerful a pain killer, and had no side effects, therefore the FDA would only allow the manufacturers to use only one tenth of their strength in these capsules. If they allowed these pills at full strength on the market, just think of the competition they would give to the drug companies.

They also stated that after you take three of these pills on an empty stomach for three weeks or so, that pain from arthritis and other ailments would cease.

Along with all of her other health problems, Martha had developed carpal tunnel. One of her doctors wanted to operate, but after she heard of the bad effects of the operation she was hesitant to have it.

I went to one of our health food stores and in one of their books I found a health doctor who recommended taking vitamin B-6.

The owner of the store said that MSM was good for it also, and that she had it in pill and a cream form to apply directly to the arms. I bought both kinds and sent them off to Martha. After a few months there was no relief for poor Martha.

I then sent Martha two boxes of the DLPA 750.

Martha had told me that her arms would pain her all day and in the night when she was sleeping she would come awake with intense pain in both arms.

It didn't take three or four weeks like the literature said because Martha's arms were in such bad shape, but a lot longer. Martha said that the pain in her arms isn't as severe during the night as it used to be, and that maybe the pain killer in the D-Phenylalanine was finally starting to take effect.

I said, Thank you Lord, Allah, Odin and all you other guys.

1994
GOUT

I have been in Alaska for 33 years. About thirty
one years ago, I went to work on a job as a carpenter. The
superintendent's name was Ed Brown. I became friends
with him and his whole family. He now lives in Tacoma,
Washington, and every time he comes up here or I go out
to Seattle, I look him up.

About six months ago, I got a telephone call from
Mike Brown, one of Ed's sons. He told me that he and his
other brother, Jeff, were up here working on a job that their
dad had. His father had bid and received a contract to
replace a lot of windows on one of the army bases.

After the initial hellos and their telling me how
their dad was doing, they remarked on how young I looked
and how spry I was for an old fart. I told them that except
for a little fish, I was now a vegetarian. I then told them
about how I had changed my style of life. I no longer
drank, smoked, and only ate a low-fat, high-carbohydrate
diet with plenty of fruits and vegetables. I told them my
cholesterol had been 260 but was now 183.

At this point, Mike told me that he had the gout.
He said it was so bad that sometimes his feet hurt so much
that he couldn't get out of bed. He said that the doctor
gave him a drug for it that helped somewhat, but that the
drug was really upsetting his stomach. I told Mike that in
one of the many health books I had read, it said that gout
is caused by eating too much protein, such as meat and
dairy products, eggs, fish, chicken, cheese, and milk. I
asked him if he ate a lot of these products. He answered
that he loved steak and ate it every chance he got. I told
him, "That is your problem right there." He asked me

what could he do for it.

I told Mike that if I had the gout, I would take some of the things I was already taking. I told him that the main thing you have to do if you have something wrong with you, be it gout, AIDS, cancer, diabetes, heart disease, or any of the other diseases running around, was to purify your blood stream. You did it by changing your diet to one like I was on and cutting out all meat, dairy products, white flour, candy, cookies, soda pop, cigarettes, alcohol, and sweets of any kind. Also, you drank only distilled water.

I also told him that in order to help purify my blood, I also took apple cider vinegar, Kyogreen, Kyolic garlic pills, and flaxseed oil. He insisted that we go to the health food store right away, that's how bad his feet were hurting him. On the way to the store, he told me that he could hardly make it through the day, and he was worried about his future ability to work.

They were out of Kyogreen so we didn't get any. For a grand total of twenty-five dollars, we purchased all our needs and returned to his apartment. When we returned to his apartment, I told him that he should take a tablespoon of the vinegar in a glass of water or juice three times a day. I told him that he should take at least six of the garlic pills a day and at least two tablespoons of the flaxseed oil a day. Flaxseed oil has a real nice taste, and I just take it by the spoonful without any mix. It also is very good for arthritis and high blood pressure.

Mike didn't waste any time measuring out the vinegar or the flaxseed oil. He just put the bottles up to his mouth and took large swallows out of each. He then swallowed six of the garlic pills at once. He told me before I left to go home that he was going to do the same thing in the morning before he went to work.

The next day Mike called me after he returned home from work. He was ecstatic. He said all of the pain in his legs had gone away and that he felt so good at work that he worked right through his lunch hour.

A few months after Mike left Alaska and returned to Tacoma, I got a telephone call from him. He told me that he now felt like a million dollars and he had no more pain in his legs. He said that he hadn't eaten any meat for a long time.

1995
Chromium Picolinate

One day I was parked beside the Bush Company, a local nightclub and number one tourist attraction, reading a book I had just picked up. The name was *Chromium Picolinate*[10].

Mike, a friend of mine whose cab was parked right behind me, came up and sat in my cab. He asked me what book was I reading now? After I showed him the cover, he asked what it was about.

I told him that it says that most people don't get enough of the trace mineral chromium. That is why they get heart attacks, diabetes, are overweight and tired all the time. I said it was also supposed to be good for hypoglycemia.

When he asked what did it do for you, I told him that it helped clean the cholesterol out of your blood vessels, and it helps you lose weight. Also, all the books said that after you lose some pounds, it's only natural that you are going to feel better and have a lot more energy.

Mike said that we needed to get some of that stuff because being cab drivers, we didn't move around enough. He added, especially now in the wintertime, when they push all the snow from the streets up on the sidewalk and we have to walk on the street where it is dangerous.

Then he said, "It looks like you have a little bit of a stomach, too, just like me." After which he said, "Why don't you pick some of that stuff up for both of us."

I told him that I had started using it already. I had read a couple of articles about it, and I just wanted to see if there was anything new in this one.

I asked him if he was diabetic. When he said no, I

told him, that's good, because people who take this stuff have to be real careful. When he asked why, I replied, "Well, since this stuff helps the pancreas make more insulin, the diabetic doesn't have to take as much of the insulin that he is now taking. He has to check his blood sugar real close, and if his sugar is down, not take too much of his doctor's insulin. If he took too much, he could get low blood sugar, and that could be dangerous." I told him that the book suggested that a diabetic check with his doctor about it and to not take more than two of the pills a day.

Well, he said he didn't have diabetes and that he was going to get some the next day. I said, good, then we could compare our results.

Then he added, "As long as I'm getting all this free advice, maybe you could help me with something about my wife. She has sinus trouble real bad and is blowing her nose all day long." I told him that the exercises that I now did cleared up my sinus trouble and that I didn't know anything about the sinuses, other than that she should not drink milk.

There is one thing I learned that might be of help to you. When he asked me what it was, I answered. Many people think that just because they have to blow their noses quite often and nothing comes out that they have sinus trouble.

I then asked him if is wife had cracks in the corners of her mouth where Canker sores also formed. When he said yes, I knew what the problem was, because I had the same problem many years before.

Those symptoms are signs that the body is suffering from a lack of vitamin A. I told him that the same thing happened to me, and after I discovered the cause and after just a short period of taking vitamin A, all symptoms of sinus trouble disappeared and the cracks and canker sores left also.

"Before I go back to my cab, there's something I wanted to ask you about," Mike added. "What do you do when you get chapped lips? This cold weather always makes my lips crack, and I've been meaning to ask you, what do you use on yours?"

I use honey. I read somewhere that they once used it to treat wounds, so I thought I'd give it a try. And it sure works for me. I find that if I put a little on before going to sleep, they are fine in the morning. Also drinking plenty of water helps.

The next time I saw Mike, he was really happy. He said that since taking that chromium picolinate and changing his eating habits a little, he had lost sixteen pounds.

I told him I know I lost some, but not how much, because I forgot to check my weight when I started it.

I told him that I was going to keep taking it because, besides all that other good stuff it helps, it also slows down the aging process.

Anytime I read that in a report of any product making that claim, I can't hardly wait to get to the health food store to get some.

I later learned through my reading that chocoholics are that way because their bodies are lacking in chromium.

On the shelf of one of the health food stores, I saw a bottle labeled "sugar control." It contained chromium picolinate and two amino acids. It was supposed to be very good for controlling the chocolate craving of chocoholics.

I told both Ann and Kay about the chromium picolinate. Ann said that she had had a hard time getting her insulin adjusted by her doctor, and since she was now regulated right, she wasn't going to take any chance with it.

Kay started using it and is very happy with the way it has helped her.

One night I had been in the Bush Company getting a cup of coffee, and I was walking back to my cab past a long line of parked cabs.

One of the cab drivers in line, a friend of Mike's, called me over. He was sitting there eating a big piece of pizza that he had taken from a box labeled Pizza Hut on the seat beside him. He also had one of those "Slurpees" that you buy at the 7-11.

He told me that he had gotten some of those pills after Mike told him about them, and although he took two a day, they were no good because they didn't work.

I told him, "I bet there is double cheese on that pizza, and I bet you eat cheeseburgers and French fries with a cola drink from McDonald's." He said, "Yeah, how did you know?" I said, "Just a wild guess." It wasn't a wild guess, for he was just a little obese.

I told him those pills don't claim to work miracles. I told him that you have to try to change your eating habits. Also, to drink plenty of water when taking them. If not, you'll find your lack of enough water will have you eating more food in order for your body to get the moisture contents of that food.

In my later reading, I found out why Ann and Kay both contracted diabetes. Years ago, anytime you opened Ann's fridge, you would see two or three liter bottles of Pepsi sitting there. Ann always had a glass of Pepsi near at hand.

Kay's husband, Cy, worked for the Coca Cola Bottling Company in Pittsburgh for many years before he retired. There were always cases of coke around their house, and Kay was quite addicted to it.

Through the books I found out that each bottle

contained nine teaspoons of sugar.

Soda pop is the number one seller in the supermarkets. Next time you're in the supermarket at the check-out line waiting for your turn, look in the shopping carts of the people around you. Just about every one of them have soda pop. No wonder so many people are contracting diabetes and that the ages of these people is getting younger and younger each year.

The next time you are walking around downtown or at the mall, take a good look at the children and teenagers that you see. You'll be surprised at how many fat ones there are, and then you'll realize what soda pop is doing to them.

1995
Eyes

One day I was at the health food store checking
out their books when this fellow nearby started talking to
me. He told me he had been looking for a copy of a book
on Ocudyne and wanted to know if I had ever seen one. I
told him no, I hadn't. I added that I now that he had
mentioned, would he tell me something about Ocudyne.
      This is what he told me. During the Second World
War the Air force had a bunch of their people stationed in
England. The ones that flew the B29s did a lot of those
night bombing raids, so that the German anti-aircraft
gunners wouldn't be able to see them so well in the dark.
The pilots always had some tea and toast with Bilberry jam
on it before they went on their raids. After the raid pilots
reported that their vision was vastly improved after eating
the jam. Some people got interested in it, they put it in a
capsule, along with a lot of things that were supposed to
help the eyes, and started selling it in the health food stores.
He said that he had heard reports that it was very good for
treating cataracts and glaucoma.
      I bought some for Martha and two of her
daughters. I hadn't heard anything about it from them.
Maybe it takes a while to work and maybe, when their
supply ran out, they just stopped taking it.
      I pop a couple of the tablets into my mouth every
once in a while and, since I started taking the mineral drink
and also taking some zinc each day, my eyes have improved
tremendously. Caution: Do not exceed 100mg a day of
zinc.
      If you ever find yourself without your glasses, here's
a little trick I do. Make a fist and bring it up to your eye.

Put your head down close to the material you want to read. Slowly unclench your fist, leaving a small hole. When you look through the hole in your fist, the eye has all of its power focused there and you can slowly but surely read.

1995
Shark Cartilage

In one of Dr. Whitaker's newsletters, he mentioned how good shark cartilage was in fighting cancer and arthritis. As soon as I read arthritis, I perked up and read the article several times. He said the distributors for it were Ocean Health Products, Inc., and that their telephone number was 1-800-477-5108.

My sister Martha has been plagued with arthritis for many years. Years ago, she had taken steroids for it, which caused her to gain much weight, and it really shocked me when I saw her that heavy.

After that, she was on Prednisone for many years. It not only didn't cure her arthritis, but after many years of use, it caused her to lose much of the strength in her muscles.

When I used to visit her, I would see in the morning the pain she was going through. I could hear her moan a little, and it seemed she was about to cry as she rubbed her shoulders and arms, trying to relieve the pain. When I asked her if she was okay, she would always reply, " Sure, nothing wrong with me." She would never admit that she was suffering — no sympathy wanted.

It was only after many years, and only within the last few, that she admitted that she was suffering. It must have been really bad for her to say that.

I called Ocean Health Products, and the girl that answered told me that in order to find out about shark cartilage, I should go to the health food store and buy the book, *Sharks Don't Get Cancer*[11]. She told me that after reading the book, I would know how to use it and that she wasn't allowed to advise me on the phone.

In the book, the author gave instructions on how to use it. I called Ocean Health Products back up and got the same girl. She told me that the cartilage came in powder and capsule form. Since the powder was cheaper, I ordered that. For about eighty-five dollars, I received fourteen ounces in a plastic jar labeled "cartilage." I saw the same product in the health food stores, but it is much cheaper by ordering it direct. The fourteen ounces were enough to get my sister through the initial heavy use of it and then quite a way into the maintenance dosage. Since her arthritis was so bad and she had had it for so long, she had to take a larger amount than usual on her maintenance dosage.

Eventually she told me that her pain in her shoulders was down about eighty percent from what it used to be.

When I later sent her Rain Forest Una de Gato, which I will talk about in the chapter under trace minerals, she told me that the pain in her shoulders had gone away completely and that the strength was returning to her muscles.

Since the cartilage also killed cancer, and if there was any in her, it would also get wiped out. That way she got two for the price of one.

Thank the Lord, Allah, Odin, and all those other guys.

1995
Food Combining

One time while I was driving my cab, I picked up two men at the Sea Galley Restaurant. They have fabulous food and are always crowded.

On the way back to the hotel, my passengers started talking. One of the men told the other that he knew that he was going to pay for eating all that food, but he couldn't help himself. He ate it anyway and was now prepared to pay for it. His buddy asked him what he meant by that. He answered that for years he suffered with bad stomach pains and indigestion every time he ate. His buddy then asked him what his doctor had to say about it. His doctor told him that he was just one of the many people in this country who had the same problems and that he was just going to have to live with it. He also told him that they sold all kinds of antacids at the drugstore.

At this point I couldn't contain myself and burst out laughing. They were startled and asked me what was the matter. I told him that he could solve his problem very easily. He asked me what I meant by that. I then replied that all he had to do was learn proper food combining. He asked what that was. I told him that all he had to do was not to eat protein and starch at the same meal. When he ate dinner, he should eat a salad, the protein, and vegetables. And that when he wanted starches, he should eat a salad, potatoes, rice, bread, pasta, and vegetables.

I explained that for the body to digest protein it makes one kind of acid and for it to digest carbohydrates it makes another kind of acid. When you mix the proteins and carbohydrates the acids cancel each other out and the food just sits there in your stomach rotting instead of being digested. The action of the stomach muscles forces the undigested food out of your stomach.

A lot of people eat an apple or some other fruit after eating protein and carbohydrates and that is the worst thing you can do. That fruit just sits there rotting and then the pain sets in.

I told him that there were many books 15 in the health food stores that contained different combinations of meals that were very tasty.

When we got to their hotel, he thanked me very much and said that he would definitely get more information on food combining. He also concluded our conversation with a very nice tip.

All of those books, with information from the diet and food combiners, has paid off.

If more people learned proper food combining, I'm sure that the stock prices of Mylanta, Tums, Rolaids, and all of those other antacids would take a big nosedive. Also, many people would be cured of their indigestion problems, flatulence, and less gas would be added to the Ozone layer.

1995
Magnetics

On my last trip to Pittsburgh I met Ken Kocinski (1-412-375-2630). He was demonstrating Nikken Magnetic products. There was a variety of products shown on the literature he had, but I was mainly interested in three of them.

There were types of seats that were supposed to bring comfort to the back and help ease the pains there. The first one looked like it was made of wool and it had tiny magnets in it to help relieve back pains and tensions while driving or just sitting down. The second was made of a material they called Therma Tech and it was supposed to provide the same relief as the first one.

Kenko Relax products consisted of five different sizes. They were about an eighth of an inch thick and were magnetized. By placing them at various parts of the body, they were supposed to bring instant relief from a variety of ailments. These ailments included migraine headaches, carpal tunnel problems, and various other aches and pains.

Magstep was the final product. It looked like Dr. Schol's inserts for the shoes that you can buy in just any drug store or supermarket around. The advertisement said that they stimulate and relax your feet as you walk.

I gave Ken my address and phone number and he said that he would get in touch with me.

In a few days I received a package from Ken. It not only contained a folder with a bunch of testimonials from various people telling of the wonders of magnetics but an application to become a salesman for the product. After reading the testimonials I was eager to try the products out on my sisters, as they had, as I have already stated, so many things wrong with them.

The brochure explained how the magnets worked. It said that when the magnet was placed against the skin it generates heat. This sent a message to the brain telling it that it was too hot at that part of the body. The brain then had the heart send extra blood to that area in order to bring the temperature there in line with the temperature in the rest of the body. This extra blood helped the aches and pains to heal faster, and it also increased circulation to those areas that the magnets were applied to.

The brochure said that Nikken products started in Japan and that they could be found in one out of every seven Japanese homes. As long as you don't wear a pace maker or automatic internal defibrillators, these products weren't supposed to hurt you. Very important, this piece of information.

One of the doctors who used it on diabetics said he had his patients try the Magsteps in their shoes for one week. If at the end of one week they weren't satisfied, he gave their money back. It increased circulation.

There were letters from doctors, podiatrists, chiropractors and such, who, after using the products, became salesmen themselves and also signed their fellow doctors up as salesmen.

Nikken operated in the same way that Amway operated. When you signed up a new salesman, you received a commission on all their future sales. This also was paid to the widow or widower after the death of the salesperson.

Ken and another fellow came to see me. I bought some of the products and told them that I would wait until I saw how they worked before signing up as a salesman. For my sister Ann, I got a pair of Magstep inserts for her shoes. She had diabetes and was always complaining about how cold her feet were because of her poor circulation. She was amazed at how fast her feet got warm and how it was so much easier to walk with the inserts.

My sister Rose, who I discuss under the chapter headed *Rose*, had among her various other ailments a bad back. It gave her so much pain that she let some doctor operate on it. She later said that, if anything, the operation made it worse. I gave Rose one of the flex magnets. It was about four inches by six inches and an eighth of an inch thick. It fits right into the small of the back, and when placed part way into your panties they are held snugly in place. It didn't take Rose long to start to marvel at the relief that the heat from the pad was giving her.

I gave Martha a pair of the Magsteps for her feet and one of those flex magnets for her back. With all her aches and pains, she needed them. She told me that when doctors look at the charts of all her past medical problems and hospital stays they shake their heads as if to say, "What is she still doing here?"

With all of these positive results, I eagerly signed up to be a salesman of Nikken products. I took some products with me and as soon as I got back to Anchorage I ordered a few more. After I started looking around I found that there were already two different companies formed that were promoting Nikken products. Boy, was I deflated. Instead of virgin territory for my first try at selling, I was facing entrenched competition. I was also depressed over my failure with Rose. That, I detail under *Rose*.

Because of being very low on money I also had to go back to driving my cab four days a week. I sold most of my inventory to some of my friends at cost just to get my money back. I kept a pair of the shoe inserts for myself as they give me energy and a feeling of buoyancy when I walked. I also kept the seat that was made of the material called Therma Tech. Driving for a living, with all of its tension and bouncing, causes most drivers to have bad backs, but that seat sure took care of all my problems.

I know that if I stayed in Pittsburgh or lived back East where Nikken products are just getting established, that selling Nikken products would be a very lucrative business to get into. Living in Alaska with all of its beauty and the lack of humidity has spoiled me and I don't think I will ever be able to leave.

If anybody ever reads this and has some problems I've mentioned here, I know getting in touch with a Nikken salesman will solve most of those problems.

The Alaska distributor of magnets is Magnetic Alternatives, 907-522-8619.

1995
Ginkgo Biloba

On one of the afternoons that I had gotten away from Rose, I drove down to spend it with Martha.

When I was with Martha, we spent a lot of time reminiscing about the good old days of long ago. One time she was trying to remember something when she said, "Damn, I wish I didn't have this darn Alzheimer's."

I replied, "I don't have Alzheimer's, I have CRS." When she asked what that was, I told her, "Can't remember shit."

Then we both admitted that we were having trouble with our memories. I said, "I wonder if Dr. G has something for that." When I called her office, her receptionist said, yes, she could help us. I then made an appointment for a few days in the future, when I could once again get away from Rose.

After the pleasantries were exchanged on our arrival in Dr. G's office, Dr. G asked Martha to tell her something about herself.

Then Martha gave an account of her hospital stays, two heart attacks, asthma and a touch of emphysema from smoking two packs of Pall Mall unfiltered cigarettes a day, to days when she had a restaurant coffee urn in her kitchen because she got tired of always having to brew a fresh pot. Dr. G got that same look on her face that many other doctors got when they looked at a chart of Martha's past medical record. It was the one that I knew she was thinking, "How come you're not dead yet?"

She then left the office and when she returned, she brought some things for us to take. There was a bottle of Ginkgo Biloba capsules, a bag of bee pollen, and a small vial labeled Bio-Oxygen.

She told us to take two of the Ginkgo pills three times a day. We were to chew on a little of the bee pollen each day for our lungs. She said that we were to put five drops of the Bio-Oxygen into a glass of water three times each day and drink it.

She told me that I should continue on six Ginkgos a day until I returned to Anchorage, and then cut back to two a day.

I don't know about Martha, but I know it has helped me. It used to be that when the dispatcher gave me an address where I was to pick up a passenger, there was no way that I would remember it. I had to write it down; otherwise, I would have to ask the dispatcher to repeat it. They didn't like that one bit.

Since taking the Ginkgo, any address that I get stays with me long after I have both picked up the passenger and dropped him off.

At the health food store I picked up an article on supplements that help fight aging.

Of course the first think mentioned was Ginkgo. One of the other things that was mentioned was Vitamin B12. They said that among older people even though they eat a healthy diet vitamin B12 deficiency is very common. After giving Ginkgo and B12 to an older test group they were able to improve their memory.

I'm sure glad that Dr. Whitaker and Cindy got me started on them some years back.

After learning about B12 I immediately sent the article and some KAL 2000 Sublingual B12 to Martha.

I read somewhere that the body only uses as much B12 as it needs and then gets rid of the extra through the kidneys, so there is no reason to worry about toxicity.

Three years before, I had been talking to sister Kay

on the phone. She told me that she had tinnitus, or ringing in the ears. I told her I would check out the health food stores.

At the health food store I told them of Kay's problem and asked if they had anything to stop the ringing. They looked into a book that they had and showed me a line that said, this product will help to stop tinnitus. It was Ginkgo, and I bought it and sent it to Kay. Some time later, Kay told me that it lessened the amount of noise in her ears.

Later, I found out the evils of meat. I knew Kay and her husband Cy both ate a lot of it every day. Kay said that the television ads were always advising people to make sure they eat a lot of meat to supply all the protein that the body needed.

Right then I realized that this little health nut had his work cut out for him. Every time I visited or talked on the phone to them, I would preach about how meat caused her tinnitus, diabetes, heart problem, and just about every other disease in this world. It was a long, hard battle, but my eloquence and repetition wore down their resistance, and they told me one day that they cut back on the meat and eat very little of it.

The little book 16 that I purchased at the health food store said that Ginkgo helped with the following:

Alzheimer's, headaches, organ transplants, asthma, tinnitus and hearing loss, impotence, circulatory disorders, eye disorders, hemorrhoids, strokes, depression, and was a free radical fighter.

In one of my later calls to Kay, she said to me, "You know, brother, dear, you were right about that meat." Since she cut down, her tinnitus had disappeared.

I thought to myself, "thank you, Lord, Allah, Odin, and all you other guys."

There's a reason I say that. I say that because everybody says that theirs is the true God. Sometimes I don't know which one to believe.

What if those people are all right and maybe these gods are all up there in heaven. If that was the case, they probably sat around arguing which one was the real one. What if, to settle the argument, they decide to take turns. Each would have one week to be the real God. He would stand at the golden gates and greet the new arrivals. After that, he would have to get at the end of the line and wait until his turn came up again.

My dad liked to gamble, and so I guess it runs in the family. Being a good gambler, I like to cover all the angles and make sure the odds are on my side.

I want to make sure that when my turn comes and I walk up to the gate, the God on duty remembers me. "Come on in, Tony," he will say. "I heard you mentioning my name often."

Ginkgo Afterthought

I have never had any training in creative writing of any kind.

One day it just popped into my head to write a book about my steps to health.

Over the many years I have taken many bingo players to and from the bingo parlors in town. We have six bingo parlors that are very busy and a lot of "Bingoholics" are around.

It just popped into my head to take all of their complaining about coming close and not winning to write a song about it.

When people got into my cab after an unsuccessful night of trying to get that one last number that they always need and were very sad and blue, I knew just the thing to cheer them up.

I would start singing my bingo song to them and they would soon be laughing and elated.

I decided to put music to it and contacted a local musician about putting music to my words. On the phone he quoted me a figure of 25 dollars an hour or 200 for the whole song.

I met him at the bar where he and his wife entertained playing western music.

As soon as he saw the song his eyes lit up and he talked me into giving him a percentage of the song for his efforts. I agreed and we are going ahead with our publishing efforts.

A few days later I decided that we needed another song to go along with the first one so sat down and in about an hour wrote another song which I called "Giddyup".

I was sitting around the house one day thinking about my last trip to the lower forty-eight and how my luck was so bad in gambling that I did while there when a song popped into my head about quitting gambling. In about an hour I had another song written.

A short time ago I awakened out of a deep sleep with an idea in my mind for a little novelty item.

In the past this has happened and I would come awake and think boy that's a good idea, but after going back to sleep and reawakening, the idea would be gone.

This time I walked over to my desk and jotted the idea down before going back to sleep.

When I awoke the notes that I had jotted down refreshed my memory of the idea.

I had a little plastic bottle about three inches high on both sides of which I wrote the instructions for the use of it.

When I showed the bottle to Erick, a friend of mine, his eyes opened wide and he said that at three or four dollars apiece I could sell a million of them.

I told him that I didn't have the finances or knowledge to distribute it but would have the idea copyrighted, then after I get this book published would go looking for a Novelty manufacturer. If he would pay me a royalty on each one sold I would be very happy, but right now I didn't have the time.

As I mentioned, I have never had any creative training or any schooling about writing books or songs, and have never shown any sign of creativity.

I wonder if that Ginkgo has opened some passages in my brain and stirred them to action. It may seem farfetched to think so but it is food for thought.

ESKIMO GIRL©
By Tony Crncic
November 1997

If your love is breaking your heart
And you see no hope in sight,
Come North to Alaska and make another start.

They say that time and distance heals all wounds,
And I'm proof of that.

I traveled up that Alcan Highway and here's what
happened to me.

I found me a pretty little Eskimo girl and I'm as
        happy as I can be.
She has dark hair, dark eyes and a very pleasing
        personality.

Now that blond haired girl
Is just a distant memory, and

My days are filled with fishing, hunting, and
        panning for gold,
And my nights are filled with bliss in the arms of
        my sweet little Eskimo.

Exercise

Everyone knows that walking is one of the best exercises there is. Most people do some form of exercise at home. Here is one that can be done quite easily, with a minimum of effort but which is very beneficial.

Stand up to do this one. Put your hands behind your thighs, and lower your chin down to your chest. Take a deep breath and push your head and whole upper body backward. At the same time, push forward on your thighs. Hold this position for six seconds. Then come to an upright position letting all of the air out of your lungs. Repeat as long as possible.

You will notice that you have to blow your nose after doing this, as your sinuses are letting out fluid.

As time goes by, you will notice that when you breathe, you are inhaling deeply. Your body is now getting the oxygen that it needs, to rid the toxins from your system. You should also notice a slight headiness. That's your brain thanking you for the increased oxygen supply. Most people take short intakes of breath, never getting all of the toxins completely out of their body.

Illnesses

Have you noticed that in the hospital room, it is the patient trying to cheer up his visitors, instead of vice-versa?

If I was a patient lying in a hospital bed, Allah forbid, I wouldn't do any of that cheering up. If someone were standing there with big mournful eyes and looked like he was figuring out whether to spend twenty-five or fifty dollars on the flowers for my funeral, I would tell him this: This is only a temporary setback for me. Soon I'll be out of here bigger and better than ever. So please take your sadness some place else. I want only happy, cheerful people around me.

If your wife gets a look as if figuring what cruise ship she was going to go on with the insurance money, tell her you want a divorce.

If you let their gloominess rub off on you, pretty soon you will get like them. You will start thinking to yourself all is lost, and your body will believe you. Your subconscious mind plays a big part in your life whether you realize it or not.

I was into self-hypnosis many years ago and it was proven that you can make your mind do anything you tell it, even cutting out the feeling of pain when you are in agony from an injury.

When you tell your mind, "Hey, I'm going to get better in a short time, and I'll be running around having a gay old time enjoying life," the mind will believe you and go to work trying to heal your body.

Have you ever noticed that sometimes when you go to bed at night with some problem on your mind, that when you open your eyes in the morning the solution is right there in the front of your mind. You get out of bed happy, with the problem solved. Your subconscious has been working on the problem all night, so that when you wake up in the morning the stress of the problem disappears with the solution. So never underestimate the power of the mind.

Odds and Ends

I've got little piles of articles and pages taken out of newspapers and medical solicitations around my apartment. There are also those little flyers that the clerks put in your bag at the health food store, and health books that I purchase there.

Whenever something that I run across catches my eye, I put it on different piles, all related to the same subject.

Now that I have written a lot of it down, I'll be able to put some of it into storage before the fire department comes in here and gives me a citation for creating a fire hazard.

There's this one big pile from those various doctors and such that I mentioned sent these letters filled with a lot of useful information.

They slipped it in alongside all these other little teasers they have there.

I think I mentioned earlier that when enough of those different bits of the same information appeared in every one of these letters, I would go to the health food store and see if they had any books written on that subject matter. This way, I was able to learn a lot more about a lot of things.

I'm going to throw that pile out, but before I do, I'm going to write down some of the things they claim.

When I have time, I'll have this to take along with me when I go to the health food store looking to learn more. I want to learn as much as I can so I can live to a ripe old age. I want to make sure that if I do live many more years, they are all filled with good health and that I have the energy to enjoy every one of them to the fullest.

Some of these are things that might suggest a book; others are just little tidbits of information:

Ginger: motion sickness and a lot more.

Broccoli has as much calcium, ounce for ounce, as milk.

Beans prevent hemorrhoids.

Brazil nuts are high in selenium. No more than two a day.

Almonds: just a few a day provide estrogen which guards against osteoporosis.

Licorice root: bronchitis and pneumonia.

Potassium: body needs a lot, and since it is nontoxic, drink as much as you want.

Soy beans: Japanese have four times less breast and prostate cancer because they use so much of it.

Wheat bran cereal: cup with skim milk helps people that have had surgery for colon cancer grow healthy new cells in colon.

Hydrogen peroxide: helps cure emphysema, pneumonia, cancer, leukemia, TB, AIDS.
OUTLAWED BY THE FDA - because it works too good.

Ocudyne: take for at least six months before consenting to cataract surgery. Check my chapter titled "Eyes."

Migraine: herb Feverfew. Also abstain from coffee, chocolate, cheese, sour cream, and MSG for a few days and see if it disappears.

Chelatin Therapy: instead of bypass surgery and angioplasty. Cheaper and gives you younger arteries.

Glucosamine Sulfate plus Chrontyne: reverses arthritis, builds new cartilage, reduces joint swelling.

L-Glutamine: cuts craving for alcohol. Amino acid.

Papaya gives immediate relief for indigestion.

Parasites.

Bad Back: put tennis ball as close to pain as you can stand. Lay on it for no more than fifteen minutes without changing position. Pain relief.

Wrinkles: vitamin C cream helps prevent wrinkles and skin cancer.

Body odor: 15-30 mg of zinc daily.

Mothers-in-law: how to rid yourself of a
troublesome one — when she isn't looking, slip a potion
into her glass made of the following:

(I stopped right there because although I could
have used this formula many years ago, it was now too late,
and I didn't want women all over the world to start
dropping like flies.)

As I mentioned earlier, please don't take this as
gospel. Now I can throw this pile away and not have to
worry about the fire department.

1996
Minerals

One day in my mailbox I found an envelope with some medical return address on it. I took it up to my apartment, opened the envelope, and found a tape inside.

The tape was by Dr. Joel D. Wallach, 1991 Nobel Prize Nominee - Medicine[12]. The doctor gave a talk on the importance of minerals in our diet. His talk was one of the most enjoyable talks that I have ever listened to.

It told of how he learned about minerals and vitamins while working as a veterinarian. He found out that cattle got more vitamins and minerals than man, and a lot of people were dying of nutritional deficiencies.

He said that man needed ninety different minerals every day, and the best way to take them so that the body would be able to absorb them was in the colloidal form.

He said that plants are not getting enough minerals because the land is being depleted, and so we are facing more and more shortages in our body unless we take minerals and vitamin supplements.

A few of the things that a lack of sufficient minerals causes are:

Pica — women start craving pickles, ice cream, and such because of the minerals they contain.

Kids eat dirt and paint trying to get minerals into their bodies.

Boron is needed to help the body retain calcium and make testosterone for men.

Selenium — if this supplement is taken, age spots disappear from inside the body also.

Zinc — lack causes loss of sense of taste, smell, sexual vigor.

Tin — baldness and eventual deafness.

Copper — lack of it causes body sagging.

Calcium — lack of it is the cause of one hundred diseases, some of which are:

Osteoporosis
Bells Palsy
Receding gums, most dental problems
High blood pressure
Kidney stones
Insomnia
Bone spurs
Cramps and twitches
PMS
Low back pain

Some of the things that he said that mineral supplements help cure are:

Vitamin E - Just about everybody knows it is good for the heart, but he said that it helps prevent and cure early signs of Alzheimer's Disease.

Vitamin C - Linus Pauling advocated using up to 10,000 units of it to help in the cure of cancer. People using this amount should cut back on its use in case of diarrhea until they find the amount the body will tolerate.

Chromium Picolinate - Good for the following: Hyperactivity in kids caused by too much sugar. Irrational behavior by adults from too much sugar.

Chromium and Vanadium are both useful in diabetes. It reverses and cures it, but it must be closely monitored. Should be used in conjunction with doctor monitoring insulin requirements.

The tape ended and I was told to call the number on the tape for additional information if I wanted it. You bet.

As soon as the tape was over, I went to a health food store to see about getting some of that Vanadium for my sister Kay. She was already using the Chromium Picolinate, and I figured it wouldn't be any trouble for her to also use it.

They sell it under the name Vanadyl, and I almost purchased it. I was waiting in the line when I glanced on the side of the bottle. There was a warning that read people using antidepressants should not use this product. I didn't buy it because I thought Kay might be using one.

At my first opportunity, I called the number listed on the tape. It was (800) 864-7730, and the girl who answered it said her name was Hope Ureste.

She told me she worked in conjunction with Dr.

Wallach in promoting the use of minerals. She said she was also affiliated with an outfit called New Vision International, and that if I would sign on as a member, I would be able to buy my minerals and other supplements through her. For a membership kit of $6.71, I would be entitled to buy them at tremendous savings.

I was already sold after listening to the tape, so she didn't have to use any salesmanship on me. I asked her if Dr. Wallach had any book available that I could get. When she told me he had one, at a cost of twenty dollars, I eagerly said put me down for one.

She then started to read down a list of products available, and as she read, I ordered as many as my budget allowed. Here is a list of my order.

2 Bottles of Essential Minerals
2 CO Q10-Neutral C
1 Fruit Juice Power - fruit in pill capsule form
1 Vegetable Juice Power - vegetables in capsule form
2 Rain Forest Una de Gato

I asked her if she would send me a few copies of Dr. Wallach's tape so that I could give them to my friends.

When the order came, I sent some of it to my sister Martha, and I kept some. Soon after I started on the liquid minerals, which come in a liquid with a delicious taste, I noticed the difference in my body.

I no longer had these urges to go to the market and buy pumpkin pies, bunches of bananas, ice cream, and such. Whenever I had those urges, I used to try to fight it, but to no avail. I had to go to the store, because my cravings wouldn't leave until I did.

Dr. Wallach's book was a treasure trove of information. It is approximately 2 inches thick, about 8 inches wide, and 12 long. It takes quite a while to read, and I look forward to returning to its pages many times in the future. It covers a variety of subjects and was worth every penny I paid for it.

Una De Gato - Cats Claw

When I placed my order with Hope Ureste for minerals, she said they had Una de Gato, and it rang a bell in my head. Although I couldn't place it, I ordered it.

I also, at that time, asked if she would send me more tapes of the one she had previously sent me by Dr. Wallach. They arrived about a day before my order of minerals and such arrived. I wanted to send them to friends so that they could benefit from them, as I had.

In the package along with the original tapes was one additional tape, and it was about Una de Gato[13]. It was very informative and enjoyable to listen to.

The speaker this time was Dr. Forest. He said Una de Gato was from the forest of Peru where the natives have been using it for years and years. Among the many things it was used for are:

Helps bacteria in the gut
Detoxification
Immune stimulation
Arthritis
Depression
Skin disorders
Psoriasis and eczema
Chronic fatigue
Widespread pain
Learning and coordination
Infections of male and female organs
Fights cancer
AIDS
Helps adrenal gland and white blood cells
Stress

He said they may work immediately or in some people take a little more time. He suggested taking six capsules of four hundred milligrams the first day, and cutting down to two a day as you improve.

After he was done, they had testimonials from people who had used Una de Gato, and here are some of the things that they said improved with its use.

Energy, bladder control, stress relief, sexual capability in man married for twenty-four years, cleared lung congestion, digestion, helped in chemotherapy after colon cancer, woman gave 15-year-old dog some, and she started acting like a young pup. Krons disease, after 3 caps a day, showed dramatic improvement after several days. Bronchial troubles gone after one week, Diverticulitis worked in one day.

When my order came, I immediately sent Martha the Una de Gato. Previously she had told me that the sharks cartilage had cut down the pain in her shoulders and upper arms by eighty percent. It was soon after she started using the Una de Gato that she told me that after all of those years of suffering, the pain was all gone. Those words were like music to my ears.

I said my usual, "Thank you, Lord, Allah, Odin, and all the rest of you guys."

1996
Cysts - Ovium

One day the address that I was sent to turned out to be a waitress that I had seen around town for a long time. Naturally the subject of health came up as we drove toward her destination.

She told me that she had been bothered by multiple cysts on her ovaries for twelve years. She said that she sure didn't want to get a hysterectomy but she was going to have to do something, because the pain was getting worse.

I told her how Mike Brown had cured his gout by changing his eating habits and by taking some supplements to purify his blood. I said that maybe if she did the same thing it might help her.

When we got to our destination she asked me if I could call her at home the next day so that we could talk some more about the change of diet and about getting some of those supplements for her. I told her certainly because the next day was my day off.

When we got together I told her the same things that I told Mike. I said that she should give up meat, white flour, sugar, candy, cookies, cigarettes, dairy, alcohol, soda pop and sweets of all kinds.

I told her how apple cider vinegar, garlic pills, and flaxseed oil worked so well together in cleaning out the impurities in the blood. They seemed to work a very potent punch when combined in daily use.

I told her that I had read that Cayenne pepper was also very good for cysts, and ovarian tumors.

As a clincher I told her about Essiac Tea. I said that since it is so good for cancer, Aids, psoriasis, and more, it should work on cysts.

When I told her that she could get all of those things for less than $75.00, she was very elated and decided to get all of them.

We went to the health food store and got Spectrums Natural apple cider vinegar, which I told her to drink two tablespoons in a glass of water or juice a day.

She also got the Kyolic non odorous garlic pills which I told her to take four to six a day.

The flaxseed oil comes in a dark bottle. This keeps the light from getting into the bottle and spoiling the oil. I told her that she should take two tablespoons a day. Since it tastes so good, I told her she could just drink it from the spoon as I did, or put it on a salad if she wanted to. I told her that she should always keep it in the fridge or it would go rancid.

On the side of the box of Cayenne pepper it recommended taking three of the pills a day.

Inside the box of Essiac Tea were instructions about cooking the tea. I told her to follow the instructions on cooking it and then keep it in her fridge at all times after that, because it would go bad if she didn't.

I told her that when she went to drink the tea, she should pour two ounces of it into a cup, and then heat up two ounces of water and mix it with the cold tea. I told her that once she makes the tea and puts it into her fridge, she shouldn't heat it up again.

I knew she wouldn't follow all the instructions I gave her about her eating, but I figured that if she at least took all of the supplements, she should have a chance to heal her cysts.

I forget the exact time it was, but I know it wasn't very long after she started using the supplements that she told me that all of her cysts were gone along with all of her pain.

    She said that she was going to keep taking the supplements and do like I did and take an ounce of Essiac Tea every few days as a preventive. She said that she was always worried about breast cancer, and that maybe the tea would help keep it away.

    I told her that the combination of the vinegar, garlic and flaxseed was good for arthritis, high blood pressure, preventing strokes by thinning out the blood, cholesterol, diabetes, liver, the kidneys, and the immune system. I'm sure it does more than what I have listed, but you get the picture of how good it is for anyone that takes it.

Asthma - MSG

I recently read in the newspaper that Congress or the FDA passed a law that said that food processors can no longer put misleading information on the backs of their products where they list the ingredients.

Some processors list MSG, but others, in an attempt to mislead the public, put other names on the ingredients. One of the main ones they use is hydrolyzed vegetable protein. Many of the products have listings such as all natural, natural flavoring or spices.

The paper listed a number of things that MSG caused and some of the allergic symptoms, some of which are: Rash, Hives, Asthma, Sneezing, Runny Noses, and headaches.

I was amazed in the next few weeks by the responses of passengers in my cab when I asked them if they had any medical problems.

Two girls told me that they had Asthma pretty bad. When I asked them if they had headaches, rashes, and ate Chinese food, their answers were all yes. They were stunned when I told them that their Asthma was probably caused by the MSG in the food they ate.

One of the girls said that she thought the rashes were caused by the arrival of her monthly female problems.

I picked up an elderly Eskimo man at a church who gave me his destination as the Alaska Native Hospital. He told me that he had gone there to pray for his wife who they had to Medi-Vac to Anchorage from Kodiak because she had a very bad attack of Asthma.

When I asked him if she had headaches, rashes, and liked Chinese food, his answers were all yes, and he also added that they had been out to a Chinese restaurant the day before her attack.

I explained to him all about MSG, and when I dropped him off at the hospital I wrote down a list of the other names that the processors put on the labeling of their food, and told him he should make sure that she avoided them in the future. He thanked me and seemed to be in a hurry to enter the hospital to give this information to the doctor. I guess doctors aren't programmed to look for MSG as a major cause of Asthma.

I picked up an elderly Eskimo woman one day and was taking her to the bingo parlor.

On the way she told me she hadn't played bingo for a while because she had a severe asthma attack and was in the hospital for six days.

When I asked her if she had headaches and rashes on her body she answered yes. Her answer to my question as to whether she ate oriental food was an emphatic yes. She said she loved it and ate it all of the time.

She was stunned when I told her that the MSG was probably the cause of her asthma.

She then said that she loved oriental food and what was she going to do now.

I told her that Carrs, our local grocery chain, had Chinese food that didn't have MSG and that many oriental restaurants advertised that they didn't use MSG.

She said that that was where she was going to get her oriental food from now on.

When I left her at the bingo parlor she thanked me several times for the information I had given her and for all the future suffering that I saved her from.

My neighbor's daughter, Janice, had come in from Yakutat about three weeks before I read the article. She was there to go to the hospital to try to find the cause of all the rashes she had all over her body. They never did find the cause and she went back to Yakutat in the same condition that she left.

She had been married to a Korean fellow, and from him, she picked up an addiction to Oriental food. Besides eating out at various Oriental restaurants, she went to the Oriental stores and took back boxes full of food on her return to Yakutat.

As soon as I read the newspaper article I realized what had caused her rashes I called her on the phone and then sent her a copy of the article.

After reading it she lost her addiction real fast. She told me that after reading the article she took it down to the local store and showed it to the clerks working there. I think it is the only grocery store in town.

She said the clerks started checking the labels of the products that they had on the shelves and were amazed at the number of products that contained MSG.

The next time she came to town, she told me that all of her rashes had gone away and the eczema on her face cleared up also.

I was driving my neighbor Lila and her girlfriend Aurora to the bingo parlor one day in my cab.

On the way Lila started talking about how nice her daughter's face was now that the horrible eczema that she had for so long had cleared up.

At this point Aurora said, "You know, I had a bad experience with MSG one time." She then added that once, after eating at an oriental restaurant in Kotzebue, she had an attack on her way out.

She then added that as she walked out the door her throat closed up on her, she couldn't hardly breath, and she fell on the ground.

She said she didn't know if she was having a heart attack or what was happening to her.

At the hospital they gave her a shot of Benedryl and kept her there until her attack subsided.

If I could run into so many people affected by MSG in my small circle, just think how many there are all over the country who are suffering because of it.

There are probably many other people in the hospitals suffering from other illnesses besides asthma that are caused by MSG since it is in so much of our food.

It is too bad doctors aren't trained to look for it when examining patients.

1997
Super Duper Energy Drink

On my recent trip to Tacoma, Washington I stayed at the home of my very good friends Ed and Charmane Brown.

Charmane, who is very much into healthful living, mixed up a concoction for her husband as she did every day. She made enough so that I could have a glass of it. It sure was tasty and really hit the spot.

A little later I decided to take a walk down to Browns Point where there was a little shopping center. I wanted to get some fresh fruit. I ate a lot of fruit on this trip out of Alaska because the fresh fruit was so much better than the cold storage fruit that we usually get.

The walk there was about a mile and a half or two and going there wasn't so bad as it was mostly downhill.

On the way back I spent a lot of time admiring the lovely scenery as I trudged up all those hills.

I guess I admired the scenery too much because after walking for quite a while I realized that I must have missed my turnoff to the Browns.

I saw a garbage man making his rounds and asked him where Upland Terrace was and he told me it was several miles back the other way.

When I got back the first thing Charmane said to me was, "What happened, you get lost? You've been gone so long."

When I admitted that I did, she asked if I was tired, since that was a lot of walking that I had done.

I told her I wasn't a bit tired as that drink she gave me had really revved up my engine. I asked her if she would give me the recipe and here it is.

1 cup apple juice
1 whole ripe banana
4 fresh strawberries
1 teaspoon blackstrap molasses
1 tablespoon Aloe Vera juice
1 tablespoon black cherry juice concentrate
1 tablespoon powdered brewers yeast
1 teaspoon bee pollen

I take this mixture fairly regularly. I also freeze a lot of strawberries so that I don't run out and when mixed in the blender they also act as ice cubes.

I sent this recipe to Martha along with the last five items on the list. She can get the others in Pittsburgh.

I told her that if this didn't put some energy into those tired old bones of hers that nothing would, and if she had any trouble with constipation that this drink would put all her worries behind her.

1997
Two to Four Week Late Remedy

A few weeks ago a friend and her three children came to stay with me while they looked around for an apartment.

The third day that she was there she asked me where the health food store was. She said that she was two weeks late with her period and that she wanted to go to the health food store and buy some herbs that she uses when she is 2 to 4 weeks late.

This is what she bought:

        Yarrow
        Marjoram
        Chamomile
        Ginger Root
        Fennel

She said that you put a heaping tablespoon of each of the herbs into three cups of water and boil for 5 minutes. This is to be drunk as soon as it gets cool enough to drink. Tastes terrible.

She also said that you should fast for about twelve hours before drinking the tea. She said that it works within twenty four hours and that it works every time.

Sure enough the next day she told me that all of her worries were over.

1997
Grape Cure

Several years ago I read a book called *The Grape Cure*[14] by Johanna Brandt. In it the author said that she cured her cancer by going on a grape fast.

She said that she had cured many cancer patients that were in the final stage of cancer by putting them on a strictly grape fast.

Many were cured in 4 to 6 weeks.

The book only cost $4.95 and since I got the incorrect impression that it was something that you try as a last resort, I told everyone that I gave the book to, that they should go on the fast when everything else failed.

Recently I gave a copy to a friend who had inoperable cancer behind her neck. I also gave a copy to the superintendent of this apartment building. She recently had an operation for colon cancer.

I got an extra copy for myself so that I could read it again.

After reading the book I decided to go on the grape fast myself so that I could see how it worked.

I fasted on plain water for two days and took an enema each day to clean my colon, just as the book said.

On the third day I started drinking pure unsweetened grape juice that I purchased at the health food store.

I purchased three different types of grapes that I also ate throughout the day.

I put most of the grapes in the freezer of my fridge and found when I ate them that they were like miniature grapecicles and were delicious. That is the main reason that I ate more than I should have. Hard to stop they were so delicious.

The book said to eat a few grapes at a time, about 3 ounces or so, eight times a day, and to eat a minimum of one pound and a maximum of four pounds.

The potassium from the grapes gave me so much energy that I had no craving for food from the very beginning of the fast.

Since I had detoxified so much by the kyogreen when I first started using it, had colonics and juice fasted with carrot juice so many times, I thought my body was pretty well cleaned out and that I wouldn't have such a bad time with this grape fast. Talk about surprises.

My body developed a slight smell which had me taking showers quite frequently. I didn't think the odor was so bad until a friend and her three children stopped by. The little girl of four said to her mother, "Mommie, he stinks."

I guess we all have been around people who give off an odor but don't realize how bad they smell.

Right then I realized just how much poison was coming out of my pores from all over my body.

The next day it got worse. I reeked so bad that I was spending more and more time in the shower.

My body was throwing out so much poison through my kidneys that when I urinated my urine had quite a stench to it.

I didn't dare go to work because my fares would probably go in one door and out the other.

The book said that you would develop aches and pains in different parts of your body and that was just from the grape juice cleaning and repairing in those parts.

That was why I didn't get excited when I started getting twinges around my heart for a whole day. I realized that it was the grape juice doing the repairing that the book promised.

I took an enema in the morning and one at night. There was so much junk that came out of me that I was constantly flushing the toilet as I sat there.

I wish that I would have checked to see what all came out of me. I only checked one time and that was after my fever went down and most of my nausea went away.

In the bowl I saw what looked like three inch pieces of string. In looking at some material on parasites that a friend had given me I came to the conclusion that it must have been tapeworms that had been in me for God knows how long a time.

In the material about parasites it said that just about everyone has them. Especially Sushi eaters and people who eat their meat rare or medium rare.

Years ago I used to love Prime Rib cooked rare with the meat still a little pink.

Little did I know that the uncooked meat that just melted in my mouth could hold so many parasites.

The book said that when you are on a grape fast you lose weight as long as the body is being cleansed and repaired. When all of that is done, you quit losing weight.

In the first six days I lost twelve pounds. I kept on the grape juice for three more days and when I didn't lose any more weight I decided that the juice must be done in repairing my body.

Since I had been on the fast for only a short time, I decided to come off of it the same way I did when I was on the carrot juice.

I ate a small salad and an apple the first day. A larger salad and two apples the second day and then more food the third day and so on.

In the book it gives a more rigid set of rules for

people who have fasted for long periods of time and it is very important to stick to that set of rules.

In 1969 I broke a bone just below my kneecap when a faulty scaffold fell apart under me, and I dropped six feet to the ground.

I was very lucky to get a good surgeon who put a pin into it, that held it together, and I didn't have any trouble with it for a long time.

A year or so ago I purchased a small trampoline and started to do some jogging on it in an effort to lose weight.

With my sedementary lifestyle of just sitting in the cab, I am constantly fighting the battle of the bulge.

I had to quit when my knee started to hurt and as time went by it started to bother me more and more.

I was just about ready to start taking Glucosamine Sulfate, which is supposed to build up joint cartilage, when I started the grape fast.

Since the fast the discomfort in my knee has decreased by at least 90 percent.

Not only do I feel better and don't have that draggy feeling that I had for so many years, but my blood pressure went down from 140 over 85 to 124 over 72.

The book said that the fast is also good for the following:

> Arthritis
> Diabetes
> Gall Stones
> Cataracts
> Ulcerated Stomach
> Syphilis
> Tuberculosis

After the superintendent read the copy of the book I gave her she wanted to try the grape fast.

The doctor had told her that if her cancer ever came back that there was nothing that they could do for her. So even after I told her of the misery that I went through she decided to go ahead.

She said that in the first five days she lost eight pounds, but in the next three days she didn't lose any and so decided that the grapes had done their work for her and so went off her fast the same way I did.

There is no way to express my surprise when she told me that she suffered none of the symptoms that I encountered. I guess the more work that needs done the more the reaction, and I may have eaten too many grapes.

After her operation for colon cancer she decided to change her lifestyle.

She readily listened to everything her sister, who is into healthful living told her.

She also started taking all the supplements I told her about, including Essiac tea.

She told me that she thought that the supplements and the Essiac tea had probably gotten most of the cancer out of her, and that the Grape fast had probably had only a little left to clean out.

My friend who has the inoperable cancer on her neck said that she is going to try the grape fast when she gets back in several weeks from her vacation.

I sent my good friend Charmaine Brown, who is a Herbalist/Iridoligest, a copy of *The Grape Cure* and my report of the effects it had on me.

She decided to try it out and, fearing the reactions that I experienced, cancelled a whole week of appointments.

She ate about three pounds of grapes a day and stayed on the fast for fifteen days during which time she lost twelve pounds.

Not only did she have a super abundance of energy but she had no adverse reactions as I had had.

She said that she had done other cleansing regimens before but this was the easiest and best one of them all, and planned to do it three or four times a year.

Besides the weight loss, the lower back pain that she had experienced for many years went away.

She also told me that I should buy a bottle of Hydrogen Peroxide which you can get at the drug store at a very low cost.

She said to put two capfuls into a big pot of water and let all your grapes, fruit, and vegetables soak in it for at least a half hour or so.

Not only does it kill all of the pesticides that the farmers use but they stay fresher and don't spoil as fast.

I know that coffee is very bad for you so I had cut down on my consumption of it. Every once in a while I would get a craving for some and would brew a cup or two.

Since the grape cure I cannot drink coffee any more. When I do I get weak and listless and all I want to do is sleep.

After the third time this happened to me, I threw all of the coffee I had left into the garbage because I don't want to go through that misery again.

Cindy, a waitress who I told about the grape cure, decided to try it. She lost ten pounds and was very happy about it.

When I told her about what coffee did to me, she said the same thing happened to her.

She said that after work she liked to relax with a drink of Kalua and coffee but now after drinking it she is deathly sick the next day. Very disappointed as she really enjoyed that drink after a hard night's work.

The author, Johanna Brandt, says that Alcoholics,

and any one addicted to the drug habit, tobacco, tea, and coffee, should be persuaded to go on the grape cure as this would wash the craving out of the body.

Wouldn't it be something if judges sentenced drug users to the grape cure instead of jail, and it rid their bodies of the cravings that drugs produce!!

It was February 16, 1998 and I was parked on the side of the Bush Company waiting for a fare to come out. As usual the parking lot was icy like a skating rink as it is every year in February.

I decided to go inside and see how many people were left and try to see if I would get a fare or if I should move to another location to look for fares.

As I started walking towards the door I hit an icy spot and my feet went flying out from under me. I came down real hard and landed on an ice ridge of several inches that had built up. I landed on my upper left-hand side of my back about three inches away from my spine. If I had landed on my spine I know I would be paralyzed today. I felt my rib cage give as I landed.

I went to the emergency room at the hospital. The x-rays didn't show any broken ribs. My urine didn't show any blood so my kidneys weren't hurt. The doctor told me that I should take deep breaths so that my lungs wouldn't get infected.

I went home and for the next fourteen days I was in excruciating pain. I took three Advils every eight hours and they helped a little.

A hiccup, burp, or cough would give me a stab of pain right below my left rib cage. A sneeze would have me doubled over in pain and just about gasping for breath.

The only way that I could sleep was by sitting up in my easy chair. When I tried to sleep in my bed, I could only lay on my back and after an hour or so it became unbearable and I would have to move back to the chair.

After the fourteenth day I got to thinking of how the Grape Cure healed my knee and Charmaine's back. I decided to go on the Cure. Didn't fast for the two days that the book said to, but just started eating nothing but grapes.

After the second day on the Cure the burning pain that I had from my left armpit down to my waist went away.

Each day more and more of the pain left. After eight days the pain got down to something I could live with, and I had an urge for food so I went off of the Grape Cure.

Got some DLPA for pain from the health food store. All of the literature says that it takes a few weeks for it to build up in your body before it starts stopping the pain.

I'm sure lucky that everything I take reacts on me right away. I know it wasn't a day or so later that it really knocked out a lot of my pain.

The reason I changed was because any of the pain killers that you buy at the drug store really mess up your liver.

On the 32nd day after my fall I went down to the Veterans Administration to see a doctor about my back.

After she examined me she said that I was very lucky. She said that my heart and lungs were okay and that the only thing I had was a banged up rib cage. She told me to keep on taking the pain killer I was taking and that eventually the pain would go away.

I then told her about how the Grape Cure had gotten rid of a lot of my pain and that I was going back on it that day.

She was amazed at what the grapes had done for

me and asked where she could get a copy of the book. I told her Roy's Health Store. She said that she was going to get a copy of it on her lunch break as she was really interested in reading it.

After the first day I noticed a lessening of the pain, and each day there was less and less of it.

After the fifth day the pain was down to where I could stop taking the pain pills. After the seventh day there was still a little bit of discomfort in my lower rib cage but it was minimal.

Besides the grapes I drank a lot of water this second and third time that I was on the Grape Cure. And I ate a lot less grapes than I did the first time.

Maybe that was the reason I didn't have such a violent reaction as I did the first time. Or maybe all of the poisons were washed out the first time.

The only side affects I had from the Advil and the DLPA was that I was sleepy all the time.

When I first fell I thought that my cab driving days were over and that it would take a very long time for me to recover.

It's hard to believe that it has only been thirty-nine days since my fall and that I am almost healed.

That grape juice is sure a miracle worker.

I put one of those flex magnets that I describe in the chapter titled *Magnets* just below my rib cage.

After two days there was still a little tenderness in the rib cage but the pain was all gone.

Alaska Law says that if you get hurt on someone's porch or property they are liable. If you get hurt on their driveway or parking lot they are not liable.

The one thing that I have learned from this experience and which I am passing on to you is this:

If you should fall in someone's driveway or parking

lot in Alaska, crawl up onto their porch or entryway and then start hollering for help.

The book has a chapter devoted to external cancers in which poultices and compresses are used.

In cases of cancer the author says to stay on the grape fast from one week to two months, but never more than two months.

She also gives instructions for getting off the fast. It is very important to follow these instructions. Not following the instructions properly can lead to severe medical problems and even death.

The grape juice is such a powerful cleanser that it cleans out all of the poisons that have accumulated in the body, and throws them into the blood stream.

This is the reason for the fever, nausea, skin eruptions and other symptoms that develop. As they are eliminated through the pores and kidneys the symptoms and fever will subside.

Persons on insulin should cut down the dosage required as their sugar test shows a decline.

People who eat foods such as meat, milk and cheese have mucus accumulate in their intestines and digestive tract. To this mucus parasites anchor themselves and feed. The grape juice washes out all of this mucus and parasites.

This mucus should be cleaned out of the system whenever any kind of disease develops as it is the probable cause of the disease.

Have your health food store order you a copy of the book if they do not have it in stock as it will show you how much the author went through and it has more details than I have covered.

If he doesn't have it in stock you can order it from:
Ehret Literature Publishing Co., Inc.
425 Saw Mill River Road

Ardsley, NY 10523
914-479-0900

I think that everyone, whether they have cancer or not, should read The Grape Cure book and take the grape fast for increasing the health of their body.

What I am surprised at is that since this grape fast does so much good, why isn't it general knowledge and why don't we see more written about it?

After all, it's been around since 1928.

1997
The Test

I'm going to end my little story by telling you about one of my nieces and her family. Her name is Eileen, and her family is the Kerrs.

I have been tempted many times to just quit trying to convert this family. Whenever I try to switch the conversation over to health, they somehow manage to switch it back again. And I have to admit that it has been frustrating at times because I know that if they would just let me keep talking, they would soon see the light.

I have had a few breakthroughs in my battle that have made me hang in there and keep trying.

One time I had managed to get the conversation turned to the dangers of eating processed foods.

I told them that if there isn't enough calcium in the body and when they eat meat, sugar, or soda pop, the body leaches the calcium from their bones in order to digest them. That's what causes osteoporosis. I kept telling and telling them that even one glassful of carrot juice had so much calcium in it, if they drank some fairly regularly, they would never have to worry about osteoporosis in their old age.

They now have a juicer, and although I don't know how often they use it, I get consolation by just knowing it is there.

The second thing is that they attached a water filter onto their water supply after I finally convinced them that the chlorine in their drinking water was what was causing all the strep throat that their girls were constantly getting.

I recently sent them some material relating to health, and in order to get them to read that material, I said there was going to be a test given on it, with some money involved. I hope that by getting them to take this test, for the money involved, some of the good stuff will sink in and may be of use to them sometime.

So with that, I'll introduce the Kerrs and get on with this final chapter:

Eileen Kerr, my niece — I nicknamed her Gypsy when she was a young girl.

George Kerr, the Irishman father — after many years of being in Alaska, you slowly change to where you become muley, stubborn, and opinionated. Since all Irishmen are born that way, George wouldn't have any trouble becoming an Alaskan.

Megan, the oldest daughter — a gentle soul, raises rabbits and loves animals so much that she refuses to eat any animal flesh.

Erin, the middle daughter — last year I told her that she was going to be very beautiful when she grew up. So that she wouldn't get too egotistical, I added, "if it weren't for that little crook you have in your nose." She immediately shot back at me, "I do not have a crook in my nose." I wonder how much time she spent in front of her mirror making sure that there wasn't any crook there.

Katelin, last but not least — like her mother, I gave her a nickname. Her I nicknamed "Cat." She is an aspiring actress, and after two minor parts in school plays, she has finally landed her first major role. She has been picked to play one of the bratty children in a local production of "Cat on a Hot Tin Roof." They sure picked the perfect girl for the part when they picked her.

Now on with the test.

Dear Kerrs,

I told you that I was going to send you a test based on the material I sent to you. Well, here it is:

Right answers to the questions are worth five dollars apiece. If you get all twenty right, you get one hundred dollars. If you miss just one, you get nothing, so think carefully before you answer. I hope you girls let George answer most of the questions, because I want to save my hundred dollars. Circle the correct answer.

1.   When people get ill, what do most of them do?
     a.   Change their lifestyle
     b.   Run to the doctor for a prescription
     c.   Shuffle off to Buffalo

2.   Which one of these juices are natural diuretics?
     a.   Cucumber, pineapple, and celery
     b.   Beer
     c.   Coke or Pepsi

3.   What is the best thing to take for ulcers?
     a.   Zantac
     b.   Tagamet
     c.   Cabbage juice

4.   What is the best treatment for cancer?
     a.   Immediate surgery
     b.   Change of diet
     c.   Wait and see if it will go away

5.   What does CO Q 10, L-Carnatine, and Cayenne Pepper do for people's hearts?
     a.   Give them energy
     b.   Make them sneeze
     c.   Takes all their energy away

6. This one is for Megan — If you were marooned on a desert island and all that you had with you were your rabbit, a chicken, and bee pollen, which would you eat first?
   a. Rabbit
   b. Chicken
   c. Bee Pollen

7. How do you avoid osteoporosis?
   a. Exercise and make sure you get a lot of calcium in your diet
   b. Eat a lot of meat, sweets, and drink a lot of soda pop
   c. Take drugs that make your bones denser

8. What happens to food that is cooked over 120 degrees?
   a. Tastes scrumptious
   b. Loses its oxygen and enzymes
   c. Turns black and George has to eat it

9. What causes asthma and bronchial troubles?
   a. Carrot juice
   b. Too much milk
   c. Eating too many rabbits

10. What happens when you eat food in the wrong combinations?
    a. You get instant energy
    b. You lose most of your energy and just want to lay on the sofa
    c. You get so much gas, that you don't have to buy any more at the service station and your car runs smoother

11. Erin: In high school, which girls do the most boys chase after?
    a. Brainy girls
    b. Blondes
    c. Cheerleaders with crooked noses

12. This is for Cat. What movie star inspired you most?
    a. Geena Davis
    b. Teri Hatcher
    c. Benji

13. What causes colon cancer?
    a. Eating too much fruits and vegetables
    b. Eating too much cooked, processed, or canned food
    c. Kissing your wife and kicking the dog, instead of vice versa

14. When should you eat fruit?
    a. Just before dinner
    b. After eating your dinner
    c. First thing in the morning with nothing else

15. Which kind of rice is best for you?
    a. White rice
    b. Brown rice
    c. No rice at all; bad for digestion

16. When recovering from disease, what food should you avoid?
    a. Refined food, white flour, caffeine, sugar, eggs, and dairy
    b. High carbohydrates such as potatoes, rice, and pasta
    c. Pizzas

17. What is good for the teeth?
    a. Drinking water that has fluoride
    b. Getting a lot of calcium into your body and staying away from soda pop, sweets, and meat
    c. Don't brush your teeth so much — just wet the brush so your mother thinks you are brushing

18. What is a colonic?
    a. An enema
    b. A Slav from Yugoslavia
    c. Irish stew

19. When you are sick, what should your attitude be?
    a. Upbeat and cheerful
    b. Sad and blue
    c. Start asking all your friends if they will be pallbearers at your funeral

20. What is the main thing that the body uses to clean out waste from its cells?
    a. Carbon Monoxide
    b. Oxygen
    c. Irish Whiskey

Well, I guess that is about all for now, so I will close. Remember what I told you about the Eskimos. They have no word for good-bye; they just say "I love you."

Uncle Tony

I haven't received a reply yet, but I have my fingers crossed. But if I do, I know what I'm going to say:
Thank you, Lord, Allah, Odin, and all the rest of you guys.

Bibliography

1. Thomas, Richard. The Essiac Report—Unknown Cancer Remedy. Published by the Alternative Treatment Information Network, 1244 Ozeta Terrace, Los Angeles, California 90069-1993, Third Edition.

2. Mindell, Dr. Earl. Garlic—The Miracle Nutrient. Published by Keats Publishing, Inc., 27 Pine St., Box 876, New Canaan, Connecticut 06840-0876, 1994.

3. Swope, Dr. Mary Ruth. Green Leaves of Barley. Published by Swope Enterprises, Inc., P. O. Box 62104, Phoenix, Arizona 85082-2104, 1987.

4. Erasmus, Udo. Fats That Heal—Fats that Kill. Published by Alive Books, 743 Fraser Park Drive, Burnaby, BC, Canada V5J 5B9, 1986.

5. Diamond, Harvey & Marilyn. Fit For Life 2. Published by Warner Books, 1271 Avenue of the Americas, New York, New York 10020.

6. D. SC. Walker N.W. Fresh Vegetable and Fruit Juices. Published by Norwalk Press, 197 N. Cortez, Suite 200, Prescott, Arizona 86301-1978.

7. Olsen, Cynthia. Tree Tea Oil. Published by Kali Press, 1991.

8. Wade, Carlson. Amino Acids Book. Published by Keats Publishing, Inc., New Canaan, Connecticut, 1985.

9. DLPA Nutrition News, P. O. Box 55279, Riverside, California 92517.

10. Passwater, Richard A., Ph.D. Chromium Picolinate. Published by Keats Publishing, Inc., 27 Pine St., Box 876, New Canaan Connecticut, 06840-0876.

11. Lane, Dr. William I. & Comac, Linda. Sharks Don't Get Cancer. Published by Avery Publishing Group, Garden City Park, New York, 1992.

12. Wallach, Dr. Joel D. Dead Doctors Don't Lie. Tape received in mail.

13. Forest, Dr. Una De Gato—Cat's Claw. Tape received in mail.

14. Brandt, Johanna. The Grape Cure. Published by Ehret Literature Publishing Co., Inc., 425 Saw Mill Road, Ardsley, New York 10523.

15. Shelton, Herbert M. Food Combining Made Easy. Published by Willow Publishing, Inc. San Antonio, Texas, 1982.

16. Richardson, Jack N.D. The Little Herb Encyclopedia. Published by Woodland Health Foods, P.O. box 160 Pleasant Grove, Utah 84062.

Far North Publishing
1317 W. Northern Lights Blvd., #624
Anchorage, Alaska 99503
1-907-258-5109
"Order a copy for a friend"
Please send me extra copies of *How I Became A Health Nut.*

Send one copy for $12.95 each
Postage/Handling: $3.00 first book + $0.50 each additional
Payment Enclosed (check or money order) $

Print Name _____
Address _____Apt.# _____
City _____State _____Zip _____

• Prices subject to change without notice

Far North Publishing
1317 W. Northern Lights Blvd., #624
Anchorage, Alaska 99503
1-907-258-5109
"Order a copy for a friend"
Please send me extra copies of *How I Became A Health Nut.*

Send one copy for $12.95 each
Postage/Handling: $3.00 first book + $0.50 each additional
Payment Enclosed (check or money order) $

Print Name _____
Address _____Apt.# _____
City _____State _____Zip _____

• Prices subject to change without notice